Global Politics in a Post-Truth Age

EDITED BY

STEPHEN MCGLINCHEY, LEO S. F. LIN, ZEYNEP SELIN BALCI
AND PATRICK VERNON

**E-INTERNATIONAL
RELATIONS
PUBLISHING**

E-International Relations
Bristol, England
2022

ISBN:
978-1-910814-65-9 (print)
978-1-910814-67-3 (eBook)

Production: Michael Tang
Cover Image: EVorona/Shutterstock

A catalogue record for this book is available from the British Library.

E-International Relations

Editor-in-Chief and Publisher: Stephen McGlinchey
Books Editor: Bill Kakenmaster

E-International Relations is the world's leading International Relations website. Our daily publications feature expert articles, reviews and interviews – as well as student learning resources. The website is run by a non-profit organisation based in Bristol, England and staffed by an all-volunteer team of students and academics. In addition to our website content, E-International Relations publishes a range of books. As E-International Relations is committed to open access in the fullest sense, free electronic versions of our books are available at https://www.e-ir.info/

Abstract

This book brings together ten chapters that reflect upon the state of global, regional and national politics in the twenty-first century within the context of post-truth. The Oxford Dictionary's definition of post-truth describes it as circumstances in which facts are less influential in shaping public opinion and political action than emotion, belief and distortion. What unites the chapters in this book, other than their focus on the meaning and nature of post-truth, is that they also consider the (supposed) erosion of many of the norms and patterns of political and social behaviour established in the second half of the twentieth century. This is especially pertinent given the rise in social media and the internet, political polarisation, and new patterns of state rivalries that harness post-truth politics. Each chapter is styled to engage with academic themes and leading-edge research, yet also to present complex ideas accessibly where possible.

Editors

Stephen McGlinchey is a Senior Lecturer of International Relations at UWE Bristol, and Editor-in-Chief and Publisher of E-International Relations. His books include *Foundations of International Relations* (Bloomsbury 2022), *International Relations Theory* (E-International Relations 2017) and *US Arms Policies Towards the Shah's Iran* (Routledge 2014).

Leo S.F. Lin is a Visiting Lecturer at the Department of International and Strategic Studies, University of Malaya, Malaysia, and a Senior Commissioning Editor at E-International Relations. He has published numerous journal articles, policy papers, and an edited book *Asia-Pacific Security: Managing Black Swans and Persistent Threats* (Springer 2018).

Zeynep Selin Balcı is PhD candidate and research assistant in International Relations at Ege University, and an Associate Articles Editor at E-International Relations. She has co-authored (with Altuğ Günal) chapters titled 'the Orthodox Church of Greece' in *Orthodox Churches and Politics in Southeastern Europe* (Palgrave Macmillan 2019) and 'Flemish Separatist Movement in Belgium' (in Turkish), in *Separatist Movements in EU* (Nobel 2020). She has also authored a chapter 'Contribution of Non-State Actors to International Environmental Law and the Relational Responsibility' (in Turkish), in *International Environmental Law and Policies* (Yetkin 2021).

Patrick Vernon is a doctoral researcher in the Department of Political Science and International Studies at the University of Birmingham, and is a Senior Commissioning Editor for E-International Relations. They are currently exploring the heteronormative dimensions of mass violence and humanitarian intervention. More broadly, they are interested in queer and feminist theory, the gendered/racialised/sexualised dimensions of global governance, and cultural figures of selfhood and/or otherness in relation to the West. They have published an article on queering genocide with *Millennium* and are a research assistant for the Jean-Monnet Network project 'Queering Post-Truth Politics: Silencing, Violence and Resistance in Online Debates about EU Integration'.

Contributors

Atal Ahmadzai holds a Ph.D. in Global Affairs from Rutgers University and is currently a Visiting Assistant Professor of International Relations. He has a diverse educational background that geographically stretches from South and Southeast Asia to North America, which covers both Western and non-Western epistemologies. His research focuses on the thematic intersection of environment-conflict-development. His publications are in the areas of human development, global governance, environment, and terrorism.

Evanthia Balla is an Assistant Professor at the University of Évora (Portugal). She directs the MA in International Relations and European Studies. She collaborates as a researcher with the Research Center in Political Science (CICP). She conducts research on European policy and security. Her recent publications include 'The Evolution of the EU's Security Model Through the Lenses of the Balkans' in *International Relations and Diplomacy* (2021). She has recently edited a book on human rights (Rocha e Cunha S., Balla E., Vasquez, R. Justiça e Direitos Humanos numa Era de transição. 2019 Húmus).

Emil Sondaj Hansen holds an MPhil in Politics and International Studies, and a BA in Human, Social and Political Sciences from the University of Cambridge. He is an Academic Officer at the Royal Danish Embassy in Berlin.

Ari-Elmeri Hyvönen works at the Academy of Finland Center of Excellence in Law, Identity and the European Narratives at the University of Helsinki. For 2022–2023, he is a Fulbright Finland Senior Visiting Scholar at Cornell University. Previously, he has acted as a Senior Lecturer of Political Science at the University of Jyväskylä and held several post-doctoral positions. He has been a visiting fellow at Bard College, New York, and the University of Verona, Italy. His work has appeared, among other places, in *Political Theory*, *European Journal of Social Theory*, *Philosophy Today*, *New Perspectives*, *Resilience,* and several edited volumes.

Theresa Man Ling Lee is an Associate Professor of Political Science at the University of Guelph (Canada). Lee is a political theorist who specializes in contemporary political thought. Her research and teaching areas include continental philosophy, Marxism and critical theory, feminism, postmodernism, philosophy of social science, psychoanalysis, multiculturalism, human rights, disability studies, modern Chinese political thought and comparative political theory. Lee has published on a wide range of subjects in these areas, including intercultural pedagogy and the challenges of teaching as a person with multiple minority designations in a Canadian university classroom.

Spiros Makris is an Associate Professor of Political Theory at the University of Macedonia, Greece and a Visiting Research Fellow at the Centre for Rights and Anti-Colonial Justice, School of Global Studies, University of Sussex, UK. His teaching, writing and research focus on issues of political ontology, political theology and post-foundational political thought.

Kyriakos Mikelis is an Assistant Professor at the University of Macedonia/ Department of International European Studies (Thessaloniki). He also teaches at the Hellenic Open University and at the Neapolis University Pafos. His degrees include a BA from the University of Macedonia, an MA from the University of Kent at Canterbury and a PhD from Panteion University (Athens). He specialises in Theory and Historiography of International Relations.

Ido Oren is Associate Professor of political science at the University of Florida. He is the author of *Our Enemies and US: America's Rivalries and the Making of Political Science* (2003, Cornell University Press) and his articles have appeared in *International Security* and *Review of International Studies*. He is a member of the Council of the American Political Science Association and a former VP of the International Studies Association. He earned a BA from Tel-Aviv University, MA from New York University, and PhD from the University of Chicago.

Silvério da Rocha-Cunha is a Professor of Political Theory at the University of Évora. He has a PhD in Legal and Political Theory from the University of Évora and is an integrated member of the Research Centre of Political Science [CICP]. He is the author of *Paradoxes of Modernity in International Political Theory* (2017, V. N. Famalicão, Húmus).

Hasmet M. Uluorta is an Associate Professor of Political Studies and International Development Studies at Trent University in Peterborough, Canada. His scholarly interests include globalisation, theories of international relations, global political economy, employment/work strategies and the socio-political impacts of new technologies. Recent research focuses on the U.S. model of development, seeking to clarify why consent may be forthcoming despite the existence of hyper-contradictions. He is currently working on a book, *The Ethical All-American and the Rise of the Probability Society* to be published by Palgrave Macmillan.

Rafael Franco Vasques has a Master's degree in International Relations and European Studies from the University of Évora and is a collaborator member of the CICP. He is the author of *Conflito e Ordem Mundial no pensamento de Carl Schmitt* (2015, Évora-Braga, CICP).

Irene Viparelli is an Assistant Professor at the University of Évora, Department of Economics, Escola de Ciências Sociais (Portugal), an Integrated Member of the Research Center CICP (Centre of Political Science.) and a PhD Collaborator of the Research Center PRAXIS (University of Beira Interior). She conducts research on Political Theory and has edited two recent books: Viparelli I., Ruoppo A. P. *Aporie dell'integrazione europea : tra universalismo umanitario e sovranismo*. (2021 FedOA Press) and Viparelli I., Rocha e Cunha S., *A crise Europeia: entre o niilismo do presente e a invenção do futuro* (2019 Humus).

Contents

1

Truth and Politics in the Age of Post-Truth

THERESA MAN LING LEE

The term post-truth is by now so ubiquitous in describing the state of politics in the Western world and even beyond that the most pressing issue of the day appears to be about making democracy work in the era of post-truth rather than questioning the normalisation of the term itself in the first place. The critical turning point appeared to have occurred in 2016 when the term was chosen by the Oxford English Dictionary as 'The Word of the Year.' On its website, the Dictionary notes the transformation of post-truth from 'being a peripheral term to being a mainstay in political commentary and connects 'the spike in frequency' directly with the Brexit referendum in the United Kingdom and the election of Donald J. Trump in the United States – both occurring in 2016. Paired with the noun 'politics,' post-truth is defined as an adjective 'relating to or denoting circumstances in which objective facts are less influential in shaping public opinion than appeals to emotion and personal belief.'

The Oxford English Dictionary traces the first use of the term to a 1992 essay in *The Nation* by the playwright Steve Tesich as he reflected on the 1980s Iran-Contra scandal and the 1990–91 Gulf War:

> We are rapidly becoming prototypes of a people that totalitarian monsters could only drool about in their dreams. All the dictators up to now have had to work hard at suppressing the truth. We, by our actions, are saying that this is no longer necessary, that we have acquired a spiritual mechanism that can denude truth of any significance. *In a very fundamental way we, as a free people, have freely decided that we want to live in some post-truth world* (Tesich 1992, 13; emphasis added).

He then continued,

> The Gulf War is over but the war at home goes on. The gulf between rich and destitute widens – between those of us who live in a modern post-industrial nation and those of us who live in the Third World countries of our inner cities. The present administration's response to this internal crisis has shifted from benign to malignant neglect. The current levels of misery and decomposition of our cities and the economic gulags of our ghettos are acceptable. Since there is only so much hope to go around, there is a freeze on hope. The have-nots have now been reclassified as never-will-haves (Tesich 1992, 13).

In the context of Tesich's essay, truth includes both facts, as in what happens, and 'moral absolutes,' as in the 'self-evident truths mentioned in our Constitution' (Tesich 1992, 14). Together, these two notions of truth entail the obligation to both act and react. The two passages cited above show that even in the early post-Cold War years, Tesich was already deeply concerned that the American people are neither prepared to act on truth nor react to truth that is disconcerting, or what he calls 'bad news' (Tesich 1992, 12). Accordingly, Tesich's insight as captured by the term post-truth is not that truth is irrelevant to what we know, but rather it is irrelevant to how we act. In contrast, 'post-truth politics,' as defined by Oxford as a term that pitches 'objective facts' against 'emotion and personal belief' such that the latter appears to have overtaken the former in shaping 'public opinion' and thereby, democratic politics. When Tesich's post-truth politics and its current usage are juxtaposed, the two are in fact not identical in terms of what truth is and how it relates to politics.

Against such consideration, this chapter provides a critical survey of selected historical events and theoretical considerations for the purpose of gaining a more nuanced understanding of the relation between truth and politics.

Truth and Language

One notable impact of post-truth politics is that language is being overtly deployed as a political weapon not only by politicians and those in power, but among the general population. It seems that once facts are irrelevant to the validity of what is being said, language becomes the platform for an all-out political contest in which what is said is no more than an act of will expressed as an assertion of power and/or an exercise in defiance.

As early as in the writings of Thucydides (460–400 BCE), the vulnerability of *logos* – which is the human capacity for rational discourse in tumultuous times – was already noted. Thucydides belonged to a school of Greek thought which maintained that language is conventional and that the association between name and things is a result of 'human use and habit' rather than 'nature or divine dispensation' (Connor 1984, 99). The conventional nature of language means that it is incapable of providing its users with any independent criteria for judgement.

In Thucydides' study of the Peloponnesian War (431–405 BCE), the subversion of *logos* as seen in the manipulation of language was introduced through his account of the civil war in Corcyra (Thucydides 1972, 236-245). The war first broke out in 427 BCE between the pro-Athenian democratic faction and the pro-Spartan oligarchic faction before it spread to the rest of the Greek world. There was a general breakdown of law and order, resulting in extreme violence and death. Language underwent changes that were reflective of the events of the time. The English philosopher Thomas Hobbes (1588–1679) translated Thucydides' description of the situation as follows:

> The received value of names imposed for signification of things, was changed into arbitrary. For inconsiderate boldness, was counted true-hearted manliness: provident deliberation, a handsome fear: modesty, the cloak of cowardice: to be wise in everything, to be lazy in everything... he that had been so provident as not to need to do the one or the other, was said to be a dissolver of society, and one that stood in fear of his adversary. In brief, he that could outstrip another in the doing of an evil act, or that could persuade another thereto that never meant it, was commended (Hobbes 1839–1845, 8: 348; Thucydides 1972, 242-243).

What concerned Thucydides most was that the meanings of words are no more than linguistic conventions that require *logos* to support them. The Corcyrean civil war was a reminder that such capacity cannot be assumed. This is why history understood as an authentic account of what happens matters. Guided by *logos*, the historian's task is 'the search after truth', which is established through 'the absence of the fabulous,' including 'the rejection of myth and unverifiable stories' (de Jonge 2017, 2). Thus, history plays an important role in facilitating the stability of language – without which distinctions and judgements cannot be rendered communicable.

Just like Thucydides, Hobbes was a nominalist who subscribed to the view that there is no inherent meaning to words. Hobbes' state of nature, where there is no common authority, is precisely one in which distinctions cannot be made. As Hobbes put it, there is 'no *Mine* and *Thine* distinct' nor is there distinction between 'the notions of Right and Wrong, Justice and Injustice' (1968, 188; emphasis in original). This is clearly an unsustainable condition for everyone. Behind Hobbes' famous words that life in the state of nature is 'solitary, poor, nasty, brutish, and short' is his uncompromising argument for the 'Leviathan', which is described by the late American political theorist, Sheldon Wolin (1922–2015), as the 'sovereign definer' (Hobbes 1968, 186; Wolin 2004, 238–243). Accordingly, the social contract is importantly a 'linguistic contract' that binds all parties to 'general names agreed upon' (Peters 1979, 125; Hobbes 1968, 111).

Through Thucydides and Hobbes, we can identify a line of thinking that sees politics as a contestation over the use of language, which is based on shared conventions and norms. Thus understood, politics is not a collective quest for the true nature of our being or an epistemological exercise in pursuit of true knowledge. Rather, politics is about humans living with one another by finding a shared language to communicate with one another on matters that affect them all. Truth is in that sense contingent on what is being said as opposed to setting the standard for it. In other words, truth is the embodiment of shareability among us. While truth as such ensures the viability of a political entity, truth by no means represents a normative standard to adjudicate among contesting actors in what they say, let alone in what they do.

During Thucydides' times, ancient China was also experiencing a tumultuous time as the ruling Zhou dynasty deteriorated into the period of the Warring States (481–221 BCE). This was when the rulers of Zhou no longer presided over the territories brought under its control through conquest. Instead of professing allegiance to the Zhou royalty, the lords of these territories became kings themselves to rule over their own land. The period was one marked by endless military campaigns as each of the seven major states aimed to conquer the rest (Lewis 1999). Yet, the period was also known for its intellectual vibrancy as different thinkers challenged the restoring of order among these warring states – including offering ideas and advice to rulers on good governance. Among these thinkers was Confucius (551–479 BCE). His thought, which came to be known as Confucianism, went on to become the state ideology of China from the Han dynasty (206 BCE–222 CE) until the end of the Qing dynasty in 1911 when China became a republic. The founding text of Confucianism was the *Analects*, which is a collection of dialogues between Confucius and his students as recorded by them.

One key concept Confucius advanced is the 'rectification of names'. Though the term only appears in one exchange in the *Analects*, it is considered a major aspect of Confucius' thought. Generations of Confucian scholars from past and present, including Western academics, have debated over its interpretation (Makeham 2003). The passage in question reads as follows:

> Zi Lu said: 'The monarch of the state of Wei wants you to govern the country, what is the first thing you plan on doing?' Confucius said: 'First it is necessary to rectify the names.' Zi Lu said: 'Is that really what has to be done? You are being too pedantic, aren't you now? How will you rectify these names?'
> Confucius said: 'Zhong You, you are too unrefined. A gentleman, faced with a matter that he does not understand, takes a skeptical attitude. If names are not correct, one cannot speak smoothly and reasonably, and if one cannot speak smoothly and reasonably, affairs cannot be managed successfully. If affairs cannot be managed successfully, rites and music will not be conducted. If rites and music are not conducted, punishments will not be suitable. And if punishments are not suitable, the common people will not know what to do. So, when the gentleman uses names, it is necessary to be able to speak so that people understand. If one can say it, one can definitely do it. A gentleman should not be careless with words' (*Analects* 13:3 in Cao 2016, 148).

This translation is offered by the contemporary philosopher Cao Feng. As Cao notes, the passage is what started the whole debate over 'exactly what kind of names did Confucius... wish to rectify' (Cao 2016, 148). Of the three major groups of interpretation examined by Cao, beginning with classical Confucian scholarship, one is arguably the most influential and certainly most pertinent to the issue of language and politics. This is the interpretation that was first associated with the Neo-Confucian master, Zhu Xi (1130–1200), who argued that the 'rectification of names is simply the rectification of politics' (Cao 2016, 149). Within this interpretive framework, rectification has the dual functions of correction and prescription by ensuring that predetermined hierarchical roles are strictly adhered to through following 'the system of rites and propriety' (Cao 2016, 151). In addition, the rectification of names entails 'using names to rectify actuality' (Cao 2016, 151). Yet Cao rejects this whole body of interpretive works by arguing that these were ideas developed later. Instead, Cao suggests the following:

> The original meaning of Confucius' rectification of names may, then, be quite simple. Confucius did not mean to establish a concrete, normative system of "names"; rather, Confucius was

simply the first person in history to realize or remark upon the importance of language in politics. As a politician, he noticed and foresaw the impact that the indeterminacy, ambiguity, and arbitrariness of names would have on politics. Confucius recognized the political consequences of language's not accurately expressing meaning or not being accurately received by people. He realized the great role that names, as a means of distinguishing right and wrong and establishing norms, could play in society and politics (Cao 2016, 168).

Scholarly debates aside, Cao's view has the advantage of identifying an interpretation of this controversial exchange in the *Analects* that enables its readers to extrapolate from it the observation that the meaning of words depends as much on their users as on their interpreters; neither of which can be predetermined. Accordingly, a good ruler is someone who can speak without ambiguity to his subjects and make good his words through actions. Stated differently, Cao's view on what concerned Confucius then, who was living through times of protracted political upheaval, is that language is an indispensable political tool for those in power and can be deployed by both good and bad rulers alike.

To sum up, this historical survey shows that politics as a war of words is by no means a distinctive marker of contemporary politics nor the Western world. Be it ancient or current, east or west, language is subject to manipulation to serve political purposes and when there is an outright war of words that defies existing norms, it is indicative of a political situation in which people no longer share a language and truth becomes irrelevant. Accordingly, political order entails stability in language use.

Truth and Politics

As previously noted, current use of the term post-truth as an adjective to the term 'politics' suggests that once there was a time when politics aligned with truth. Indeed, if we start with Plato's *Republic* as the key founding text of Western political thought, we see that the ideal *polis* (city-state of ancient Greece) is where truth and politics converge, and justice is achieved. Written around 380 BCE when Athens was still coping with its defeat by the Spartans in the Peloponnesian War, the *Republic* is a defence of the rule of the 'philosopher king', defined as someone who is 'guided by the truth' and is 'always and in every way' in pursuit of the truth (Plato 1974, 490a). For Plato, truth converges with virtues and hence, letting the philosopher take charge of politics is to let the wisest and the most virtuous lead the less wise and the less virtuous even if it requires compulsion (Plato 1974, 499b). In Plato's words, '...until the philosophers attain power in a city there will be no respite from evil for either city or citizens...' (Plato 1974, 501e). The uncompromising rule of philosopher-kings is made palatable by the claim that we are all 'earth-born brothers' with random mixtures of gold, silver, bronze and iron, but only the gold can rule (Plato 1974, 414–415).

Understandably, academic debates over the interpretation of Plato's *Republic* revolve around the question of whether truth as attained in philosophy can be realised in politics as action and whether such a connection is even desirable. Without getting into the details of these scholarly exchanges, I suggest that they all share the concern that truth acquired through the rigorous process of philosophical reasoning is not without problem when applied to the real world of living humans. This is because not all humans are philosophers – and indeed, in Plato's view, not everyone is capable of becoming a philosopher given the protracted and arduous training that one needs to endure to become one. Hannah Arendt (1906–1975), a highly influential political philosopher of the twentieth century, notes that 'Plato was the first to introduce the division between those who know and do not act and those who act and do not know' and that such a separation has remained 'at the root of all theories of domination' (Arendt 1958, 223, 225). What Arendt points out in this remark is not the gap between theory and practice, but rather that Plato provides the normative ground for those who know the truth to tell those who do not know what to do.

Arendt herself took on the challenge of understanding the relationship between truth and politics through her analysis of Nazism and Stalinism. Arendt's insight, which was controversial when *The Origins of Totalitarianism* was published in 1951, was to identify Nazism and Stalinism as representative of a new form of political rule – totalitarianism – making it distinct from 'other forms of political oppression... such as despotism, tyranny and dictatorship' (Arendt 1973, 460). Arendt defines totalitarianism as a self-contained system of ideas driven by their 'logic' and marked by a mode of reasoning called 'ideological thinking.' Ideological thinking as such is a distinctive form of political reasoning defined by three characteristics. First, ideological thinking claims to provide a 'total explanation' of all historical happenings, encompassing the past, the present, and the future. Second, while ideological thinking is an attempt to account for 'factual reality' in its totality, this mode of thinking is paradoxically divorced from reality and experience. This is because experience, being rooted in specificity, is clearly limited in its claim to totality. It follows that as its third characteristic, ideological thinking aims to emancipate thought from the limitation imposed by experience through a 'specific method of demonstration.' The method involves arranging facts into an 'absolutely logical procedure' that starts from an 'axiomatically accepted premise'. It is, in short, a 'process of deduction from a premise' – which is the only possible movement in the realm of logic that leads to one definitive conclusion. This is how the 'logicality of ideological thinking' provides the basis for total explanation and the 'principle of action' for totalitarian movement (Arendt 1973, 468–474).

Stated differently, totalitarianism is a form of uncompromising idealism that exists in one's head irrespective of shared reality as experienced. It is the perverse form of what Arendt later refers to as 'rational truth', which is the product of the 'speculative mind' that belongs to philosophy, mathematics and the sciences. The 'speculative mind' is the mind working on its way to generate axioms and theories by relying on the cognitive capacity of the human brain (Arendt 1977, 231). The presence of others has no bearing whatsoever on rational truth. In contrast, 'factual truth' is what happens when humans are 'living and acting together' (Arendt 1977, 231). Factual truth is therefore particular and temporal by definition. But more importantly, factual truth is 'political by nature' because it can only be validated in the context of the human community (Arendt 1977, 238). In other words, factual truth is about humans in their plurality rather than in their singularity. For factual truth to be sustainable, we need what Arendt calls 'common sense' – understood as 'community sense' (Arendt 1982, 72).

There is also another distinction about truth that Arendt makes which is pertinent to understanding how totalitarianism works. The issue is whether the so-called totalitarian ideology is simply an unnecessarily cumbersome way of saying that it is an all-round and polished lie. Here, Arendt calls totalitarian ideology the 'modern lie' – in contrast to the 'traditional lie'. The latter is restricted by two conditions: that it is a lie about the 'particulars' and that it deceives only the 'enemy' – which means that the liar is not engaged in self-deception. The modern lie, however, involves a 'complete rearrangement of the whole factual texture'. It also intends to deceive everyone alike, to the extent that those who initiate the lie eventually 'fall victims to their own falsehood' (Arendt 1977, 249–254).

This distinction between the traditional and modern lie is important. It indicates that not only is totalitarianism a lie, but the lie is in fact too big to fit into the standard meaning of the word. To tell a lie from truth, we need a common standard. In the case of a traditional lie, the common standard is precisely 'the fabric of factuality'. As such, a lie always appears as a 'tear' to that fabric. Yet, modern lies require making a surrogate reality with a completely different context for facts to fit 'without seam, crack, or fissure, exactly as the facts fitted into their original context'. Arendt notes that as long as those who concoct the surrogate reality are prepared to engage in self-deception to 'create a semblance of truthfulness', there is nothing to prevent 'these new stories, images, and non-facts from becoming an adequate substitute for reality and factuality' (Arendt 1977, 253–254).

Totalitarianism therefore requires a person to stand outside of the system itself in order to make sense of it. Arendt points out that it is futile for us to argue with (for example) a Nazi or a Stalinist on race or class. To confront totalitarianism requires more than just a confrontation with specific facts. It is a more fundamental confrontation between reality as experienced and its total rejection. This means that Nazism and Stalinism are more than radical ways of conducting racial conflict or class struggle. Rather:

> Totalitarian politics – far from being simply antisemitic or racist or imperialist or communist – use and abuse their own ideological and political elements until the basis of factual reality, from which the ideologies originally derived their propaganda value– the value of struggle, for instance, or the interest conflicts between Jews and their neighbours – have all but disappeared (Arendt 1973, xv).

Accordingly:

> The ideal subject of totalitarian rule is not the convinced Nazi or the convinced Communist, but people for whom the distinction between fact and fiction (that is, the reality of experience) and the distinction between true and false (that is, the standards of thought) no longer exist (Arendt 1973, 474).

Who then is the 'ideal subject' of totalitarianism? Although there is a revival of interest in Arendt's observation on truth and politics since the onset of post-truth politics, not enough has been said about her reply to the question (Hyvönen 2018; Klinkler 2018; Lee 2019; Zerilli 2020). Yet if we take a look at Arendt's portrait of this ideal subject, her view is even more pertinent to our current challenge.

As a self-contained system of ideas that is detached from experience, totalitarian thinking offers consistency in ways that reality cannot. Arendt notes that this kind of consistency is especially appealing to those who have lost a sense of bearing in the world (Arendt 1973, 353). They constitute what she calls the 'masses'. The 'mass man' is thus a highly isolated and atomised individual, who is 'obsessed by a desire to escape from reality' (Arendt 1973, 318, 352). In his 'essential homelessness' the mass man can 'no longer bear its accidental, incomprehensible aspects' (Arendt 1973, 352). This longing for escape from reality is a 'verdict against the world' in which one is 'forced to live' but 'cannot exist' (Arendt 1973, 352). Such a situation is ripe for the 'revolt of the masses' against 'common sense,' which is 'the result of their atomisation, of their loss of social status' and with it, the 'whole sector of communal relationships in whose framework common sense makes sense' (Arendt 1973, 352). In short, the masses are people who are considered to be 'superfluous or can be spared … [who] cannot be integrated into any organisation based on common interest' (Arendt 1973, 311).

Whether one agrees with Arendt's analysis of the social conditions in the interwar years that led to the formation of the 'masses', her portrait of the 'mass man' is a powerful account of what can happen to an individual who has become disposable to the society that they used to belong to. Hand in hand with this phenomenon is indeed the collapse of 'common sense' that leaves the dislodged individual scrambling for reconnection. By offering the masses a substitute reality validated by the 'logic of an idea' rather than by experience, totalitarianism makes it possible for them to live in a world where there is no condition of plurality. Between 'facing the anarchic growth and total arbitrariness of decay' and 'bowing down before the most rigid, fantastically fictitious consistency of an ideology', the masses will likely 'choose the latter' (Arendt 1973, 352). A world created by ideology, then, is more attractive to the masses not because 'they are stupid and wicked, but because in the general disaster this escape grants them a minimum of self-respect' by conjuring up 'a lying world of consistency which is more adequate to the needs of the human mind than reality itself' (Arendt 1973, 353). Moreover, it is precisely this ability to guarantee consistency that makes it possible for the leaders of totalitarian movements to demand 'total, unrestricted, unconditional and unalterable loyalty of the individual member' (Arendt 1973, 323).

While this chapter is not a study of the social factors that led to specific contemporary developments such as the result of the Brexit referendum or the election of Donald Trump in 2016, Arendt's 'mass man' seem to have found their counterparts among the supporters of Brexit and Trumpism. Studies of voters' profiles in both events point to a disproportionate share of supporters from white male lower income backgrounds without university educations. These are individuals who have either already lost their jobs to globalisation or who are at high risk of losing their job with very little capacity to be retrained for the twenty-first century market economy of advanced industrialised states (BBC 2016; Pew Research Center 2018). In short, these displaced workers are part of the tapestry forming the modern equivalent of Arendt's 'mass man' – ready to be the recruits of totalitarianism.

Conclusion

If we step back to take a more comprehensive approach to the relationship between truth and politics, both historically and theoretically, it is not so obvious that 2016 is a defining moment. From ancient China and ancient Greece to our so-called post-truth age, the indeterminacy of language appears to be a persistent political challenge. Language is always open to manipulation by its users to serve power. Nonetheless, the tendency these days is to single out the ubiquity of social media and the proliferation of Internet platforms as the incubator for the countless cyberwars of words that in turn fuel the real world of politics. In this context, language is no longer the conveyor of objective facts and accurate information, but rather the medium for expressing subjective opinions and feelings, as captured by the Oxford Dictionary's definition of the term 'post-truth politics'.

In contrast, the historical approach used in this chapter shows that it is in fact too easy to point the figure at the Internet and digital communication for the political challenge that we face today. What is being suggested here is that with or without the Internet, language, be it used to convey facts or emotions, is simply a tool for communication that humans have invented. While language per se cannot adjudicate what is true or not true, what is right or wrong, it embodies such capacity when language is a shared norm. That shared norm cannot be sustained without some semblance of cohesion in any given community. Any war of words, irrespective of its platform, is indicative of the breakdown of such cohesiveness.

Returning to the original context in which the term post-truth politics was first used by Steve Tesich helps to identify the important distinction between truth as the standard for knowledge and truth as the standard for action. The two do not necessarily coincide. Placed in the context of the history of political thought, this distinction is in fact at the heart of Plato's *Republic*. Yet when the philosopher as the quintessential bearer of truth becomes king, the *polis* that he rules over is far from the ideal of a just state that it purports to be. Instead, it is one that is held together by lies and coercion. What Arendt reveals through her study of Nazism and Stalinism is that it is dangerous for the kind of truth that philosophy generates – 'rational truth' – to become the guide to politics. Politics guided by rational truth can only be uncompromising and follows a logic of its own that cannot afford the ambiguity and indeterminacy of reality as lived experiences of humans.

A world of post-truth politics can be an opportunity for a new kind of politics if it is indeed about dismantling the idea that truth is the ideal that politics should strive for. But as it stands, the post-truth politics of today is more about invoking a past that never exists to judge the presence as a crisis in naming when the real crisis is about rebuilding a shared space that has room for all – be they of the left, right or centre; cosmopolitan or parochial; civic-minded or self-centred; liberal-minded or bigoted. Politics is and always will be about striving for that space, without which no human can thrive.

References

Arendt, Hannah. 1958. *The Human Condition*. Chicago: The University of Chicago Press.

Arendt, Hannah. 1973. *The Origins of Totalitarianism*. Rev. ed. New York: Harcourt Brace Jovanovich.

Arendt, Hannah. 1977. "Truth and Politics." In *Between Past and Future*, 227–264. New York: Penguin Books.

Arendt, Hannah. 1982. *Lectures on Kant's Political Philosophy*, edited by Ronald Beiner. Chicago: University of Chicago Press.

British Broadcasting Corporation. 2016. "Brexit vote: The breakdown." BBC News, December 7, 2016. https://www.bbc.com/news/uk-politics-38227674

Cao, Feng. 2016. "A New Examination of Confucius' Rectification of Names." *Journal of Chinese Humanities* 2: 147–171. https://doi-org.subzero.lib. uoguelph.ca/ doi/ 10.1163/23521341-12340032.

Connor, W. Robert. 1984. *Thucydides*. Princeton: Princeton University Press.

de Jonge, Casper C. 2017. "Dionysius of Halicarnassus on Thucydides." in *The Oxford Handbook of Thucydides*, edited by Sara Forsdyke, Edith Foster, and Ryan Balot. Oxford University Press. DOI: 10.1093/ oxfordhb/9780199340385.013.17 https://www-oxfordhandbooks-com.subzero. lib.uoguelph.ca/view/10.1093/oxfordhb/9780199340385.001.0001/ oxfordhb-9780199340385

Hyvönen, Ari-Elmeri. 2018. "Careless Speech: Conceptualizing Post-Truth Politics." *New Perspectives* 26 (3): 31–55. https://www.proquest.com/ scholarly-journals/careless-speech-conceptualizing-post-truth/ docview/2204515132/se-2?accountid=11233.

Hobbes, Thomas. 1839–1845. *The English Works of Thomas Hobbes*, edited by Sir William Molesworth. London: John Bohn. Vol. 8.

Klinkner, Melanie. 2018. "Reasonable Truth." *International Journal of Media & Cultural Politics* 14 (3): 393–99. doi:10.1386/macp.14.3.393_7.

Lee, Haiyan. 2019. "When Nothing Is True, Everything Is Possible: On Truth and Power by Way of Socialist Realism." *PMLA/Publications of the Modern Language Association of America* 134 (5). Cambridge University Press: 1157–64. https://doi.org/10.1632/pmla.2019.134.5.1157

Lewis, Mark E. 1999. "Warring States Political History." In *The Cambridge History of Ancient China: From the Origins of Civilization to 221 BC*, edited by Michael Loewe and Edward Shaughnessy, 587–650. Cambridge: Cambridge University Press.

Makeham, John. 2003. "Zheng ming (Rectification of names)." In *RoutledgeCurzon Encyclopedia of Confucianism*, edited by Xinzhong Yao. Vol. 2: 813-814. New York: Routledge.

Oxford Languages, n. d. "Word of the Year 2016." Accessed 19 August 2017. https://languages.oup.com/word-of-the-year/2016/

Peters, Richard. 1979. *Hobbes*. Westport: Greenwood Press.

Pew Research Center. 2018. "An examination of the 2016 electorate, based on validated voters." *Report*, August 9, 2018. https://www.pewresearch.org/politics/2018/08/09/an-examination-of-the-2016-electorate-based-on-validated-voters/

Plato. 1974. *Republic*. Translated by G. M. A. Grube. Indianapolis: Hackett.

Tesich, Steve. 1992. "Watergate Syndrome: A Government of Lies." *The Nation*: 12-14. January 6/13, 1992.

Thucydides. 1972. *The Peloponnesian War*. Translated by Rex Warner. Harmondsworth, England: Penguin Books.

Wolin, Sheldon. 2004. *Politics and Vision: Continuity and Innovation in Westen Political Thought*. Expanded Edition. Princeton: Princeton University Press.

Zerilli, Linda M. G. 2020. 'Fact-Checking and Truth-Telling in an Age of Alternative Facts.' *Le foucaldien* 6, no. 1: 2, 1–22.

2

Platforms of Post-Truth: Outlines of a Structural Transformation of the Public Sphere

ARI-ELMERI HYVÖNEN

On 6 January 2021, a violent mob stormed the United States Capitol Hill in an attempt to stop the US Congress from formalising the victory of Joe Biden in the November 2020 presidential election. A shock test of democratic institutions in the US, the events also represent a watershed moment in the analysis of post-truth politics that has been ongoing since the British 'Brexit' vote and the election of President Donald Trump in 2016. The acts witnessed on 6 January were incited by Trump, who in the preceding weeks had repeatedly made unfounded references to a 'stolen election'. Adding fuel to the fire were many claims about widespread election fraud in social media. The riot itself was also planned on social media, including on public Facebook pages. Many insurrectionists taking part in the events on Capitol Hill were believers of the conspiracy theory known as QAnon. Originating in the anonymous imageboard 4chan, QAnon orbits around the idea of Trump's secret battle against a cabalist elite of media, scholars, and (Democratic) politicians. While neither Trump insisting on blatant falsehoods nor the role of social media in the diffusion of misinformation was new, the events in Washington seemed to prove for the first time how severe consequences these untruths could have. Slightly less drastically, a related point was made by President Biden six months later, when he accused Facebook of 'killing people' due to its failure to stem disinformation about Covid-19 (Kanno-Youngs and Kang 2021). In both cases, it was apparent that widely spread disinformation could affect not only the behaviour of citizens online, but also lead to physical consequences, even violence, and endanger democratic processes.

This chapter seeks to shed light on the structural conditions of post-truth politics – in particular, the emergence over the last decade of social media as a central platform of public discourse. I first clarify my take on the concept of post-truth, and how it differs from various forms of mendacity that have traditionally appeared in the democratic public sphere. I highlight two aspects in the post-truth phenomena – a rhetorical style I call 'careless speech' and a broader set of structural conditions that contribute to the devaluation of factual truth. I also introduce the metaphoric vocabulary of public and factual infrastructure/architecture that forms the backbone of my analysis. The rest of the chapter then inquires into the structural transformation of the public sphere, linking the role of platform capitalism to the tension-ridden history of privately-owned public fora.

Social media is capable, perhaps more than we realise, of 'changing the ways that we act, perceive, feel, think, and live together' (Han 2017, ix). But, technologies are never autonomous actors. Their meanings and repercussions emerge from the broader political, economic, and cultural environment. Hence, I will focus on the nature of platform capitalism as a part of a broader set of developments that constitute a threat to the prerequisites of democratic politics.

On truth and democracy

After being selected the word of the year in 2016 by the Oxford English Dictionary and by Gesellschaft für deutsche Sprache, much has been written on post-truth and post-factuality. Political discussion has purportedly undergone a profound change and left facts and truth behind for good. The definition offered by the two dictionaries refers to the tyranny of emotions over cold facts. Many take a different stance altogether. Politics, especially democratic politics, is supposed to be about opinions and ideological struggle, so why worry about truth? Are we not projecting an imaginary golden age into the past, a time when truth reigned supreme? Moreover, what is truth except a petrified outcome of past political struggles? Is not the whole alleged crisis of truth and expertise merely a reflection of problematic melancholia for the waning (neo)liberal consensus of the post-Cold War era?

Let us address these concerns first from the viewpoint of democracy. A broadly accepted tenet in democratic theory is that democracy is an opinion-based form of government. However, as Nadia Urbinati argues, opinions are always 'interpretations of specific facts and events' (Urbinati 2014, 35). An exchange of opinions becomes a mere battle of forces if the opinions lack any point of reference outside themselves. Thus, as Hannah Arendt wrote, freedom of opinion means nothing if factual information is not guaranteed. Opinions, inspired by different interests, values, and emotions come in a plurality of shapes. Without anchorage in facts, their interaction is rendered into violent clash of passions (Arendt 2006, 234–237). At best, pluralistic democratic debate enhances our understanding of the shared world from various angles. A disagreement over the facts divides this shared ground into separate islands, inhabited by people distrustful of each other.

As this formulation suggests, the dictionary definitions of post-truth tend to downplay the legitimate role of emotions in politics, while the sceptics underestimate the need for shared factual ground in democratic debate. As such, the two stances reflect the poles often at play in the contemporary public sphere. On the one hand, there is a pronounced tendency to dissolve every factual question into a matter of opinion – hence destabilising the public sphere by depriving it of any common points of reference. On the other hand, an opposite but equally real threat to democracy is the attempt to reduce even legitimate disagreements to factual questions, thus subjecting them to the tribunal of expert knowledge.

I find it useful to compare factual truth to the physical infrastructure that colours our everyday experience. Life in a city, for instance, is enabled, guided, and limited by urban architecture and infrastructure. Which modes of transportation are available for my trip to uptown? Which spaces are open to the public, and which are private? In politics, we are similarly limited and enabled by a variety of tangible and intangible infrastructures and architectures.

Facts are one such enabling constraint, a limitation that at the same time facilitates, encourages and stimulates debate. This infrastructure is given form by various architectures, such as ways of accessing information. Like public infrastructure, the factual infrastructure of politics deteriorates, becomes meaningless, unless we constantly attend to it and make sense of it from our varying perspectives. No one would expect exact guidelines on what to do from the material environment, just as no one would completely ignore its limitations on our actions. Finally, urban architecture may very well support racist, sexist, classist, or ableist structures of domination, and often upholds ecologically unsustainable petroculture. Yet, few would find razing the city a plausible solution to these shortcomings – the task is to restructure, not to destruct.

It is worth noting that this conceptualisation does not hinge on any particular theory of truth. Because it approaches truth politically, and not epistemologically, it is equally compatible with critical realism and non-realist approaches. Any consideration of truth in politics has to acknowledge that truth never stands on its own feet in the plural world of public affairs. The 'truthlikeness' of scientific statements, highlighted by realists, is of little value if they are ignored in political decision-making. The non-realists, in turn, often conceive truth as 'warranted assertability' – or 'what our peers will [...] let us get away with saying' (Rorty 1981, 176). The current political crisis indicates that such communities of justification are dispersing fast. Accepting what is an undisputed fact in the scientific community becomes, ironically, an indication of having failed to 'do your own research' in many online communities.

Post-truth politics, then, ought to be understood as a predicament in which the factual infrastructure is crumbling, while political speech continues to find new ways of detaching itself from it. Consequently, our ability to react to political events and to engage in a democratic process of opinion-formation is compromised. This definition combines a structural perspective with a viewpoint focused on a particular rhetorical style. The latter I call 'careless speech', by which I mean speech that not only does not care about truth, but also often does not devote any careful attention to the details of the untruths it contains. Unlike the classical lie, careless speech does not primarily serve to hide particular facts from view. It seeks to actively eliminate factuality from the criteria used to assess political opinions and decisions. It denotes the purposeful creation of ambiguity over whether people believe in the factuality of the things they say. Nothing is to be taken too seriously or literally. While available to all, careless speech is particularly forthcoming to white male politicians prone to masculine boasting and aggression. Amplifying these post-truth tendencies indicates an attitude of not caring about the democratic process, or the world we share with others (see Hyvönen 2018).

The structural transformation of the public sphere

To understand the erosion of factual infrastructure and the emergence of careless speech, these phenomena must be placed in a historical context. One particularly helpful tool for gaining such historical vantage point is Habermas's 1962 work *The Structural Transformation of the Public Sphere*. Particularly when combined with later correctives and elaborations, the book is an indispensable resource for the critique of 'actually existing democracy', also in the digital sphere (Fraser 1990, 56; Wischmeyer 2019).

Habermas's historical presentation revolves around the rebirth of the public from the seventeenth century onwards. The architecture around which the modern European public emerged was mostly privately owned – salons, coffeehouses, and later the pages of newspapers. In these spaces, private people could 'come together as a public', disregarding the exact societal status of the participants. At the centre of such public sphere was the critical assessment and evaluation, exercised by private persons, of matters of public interest (Habermas 1991, 27–36, 52, 158–164). As Rosenfeld has also argued, many of the ideals regarding fact-based public debate we take for granted, such as objective news reporting, emerged only in the modern public sphere, supported by Enlightenment values (Rosenfeld 2018, 10, 25–35).

The public architecture Habermas describes – not unrelated to the point made earlier about urban infrastructure – was largely premised on exclusions based on gender, race, and class status. The disregarding of social rank only applied within the cohort of white property-owning males and did not include women, colonial subjects or the poor. To a large extent, these structures of domination continue to be coded (both metaphorically and literally) into the architectures of contemporary public spaces, amplifying the voices of traditionally dominant groups over those of the oppressed. A different historical narrative could be told by focusing on the aspects of modern publicity ignored by Habermas, such as the physical assemblies that occasionally destabilise such exclusions. But, to understand the role of media platforms in the emergence of post-truth politics, it makes sense to follow in Habermas' footsteps and trace historically the vicissitudes of privately-owned public spaces.

Importantly, Habermas's narrative points towards an aspect in modern publicity loaded with irony. What started out as a form of protection from the state authorities – private ownership – has become a threat to 'the critical functions of publicist institutions' (Habermas 1991, 188). As physical publics wither, and the media becomes increasingly driven by advertising interests, passive consumption begins to replace critical public debate (Habermas 1991, 188, 159). In the twentieth century, Habermas argues, 'the rational debate of private people becomes one of the production numbers of the stars in radio and television, a saleable package ready for the box office; it assumes commodity form' (Habermas 1991, 164).

As we will see, Habermas' history is crucial for democratic thought still today, as the shift in the fortunes, for the public, of privately-owned public spaces still defines our politics. Perceptive to what was to come, Habermas highlighted the emergence and increasing dominance of entertainment as a result of the aforementioned processes. Pivotally for us, entertainment by nature represents a shift away from fact-based debate, and 'instead of doing justice to reality, tends to present a substitute more palatable for consumption' (Habermas 1991, 170).

In the twenty years that followed the publication of *The Structural Transformation of the Public Sphere*, Habermas's ruminations about entertainment gathered more weight as television established its role as the dominant medium for daily consumption. It thus makes sense to read Neil Postman's *Amusing Ourselves to Death: Public Discourse in the Age of Show Business* (1985) as something of a sequel to Habermas's work on structural transformation – although this connection is not intended by either author. Postman's focus lies on the tendency of television to turn everything into entertainment. For him, the dominant medium, whether printing press or TV, is not a passive machine – it is a structure for discourse. As such structure, TV by its very nature tends to fragmentise and trivialise all content. (Postman 2005, 43, 87).

Although the tendency has been present from the early years of television, there have also been radical changes over the past decades. First, while early TV channels had entertainment programmes, these were supposed to finance the economically less profitable news, which in turn granted credence to the network. From the late 1970s onwards, cable news, the 24-hour news cycle, and the idea of making a profit from news have turned news themselves into entertainment – hence further eroding the distinction between facts, opinions, and fictions (See McIntyre 2018, 63–65).

More recently, the financial struggles of the television networks have pressed them to develop a distinct and marketable brand. A run-of-the-mill aspect in the marketing of ordinary consumer products, brand differentiation in news and information is arguably alarming. According to his own testimony, Cass Sunstein thinks about the economy in terms mostly owing to the neoclassical Chicago school. Yet, even from this perspective it seems clear that 'serious problems' emerge when information is treated as a consumer good among others (Sunstein 2018, 149). The goal has shifted from offending the least number of viewers to creating outrage on purpose. One of the best ways to achieve this in an entertaining way is to include 'panels of celebrity anchors and paid provocateurs making themselves, and their outrage, the "story" rather than the events they are discussing' (Tanguay 2019, 28–30).

The triumph of candidates like Trump in the 2016 US presidential elections was dependent on news media that had become completely infused in the logic of reality television. News, reformatted after the model of reality TV and the attention economy, operate in 'truth markets' where the operational logic is not driven by public interest of any kind, but by ratings. Brazenness and frequency of lies, accompanied by sexists and racist proclamations that would have been out of bounds still a decade ago were turned into a recipe for success. They grasped the attention of radicals, while the more moderate supporters were not scared away by them because the reality TV-infused media logic hollowed them out and made them seem less real (Tanguay 2019, 23–24, 30–31).

Of course, the transformation of the media is not the sole culprit. A fuller picture of the developments culminating in post-truth politics would have to account for the impact of broader trends of democratic backsliding and erosion of representative institutions over the past decades, and the phenomenon of toxic white masculinity (Bennett and Livingston 2020). For example, the 1990s consensus around liberal democratic market society effectively narrowed the space for meaningful political disagreements or policy differences of elected governments. One consequence of this was that parties became increasingly reliant on public relations agencies and outright bullshit – 'empty words you could hear anywhere' but attract 'no real believers' (Spicer 2018; Frankfurt 2005). Combined with media transformations, the general decline of social trust, thirty decades of neoliberalism, the shocks of the 2008 financial crash and other factors, the widespread use of bullshit fertilised the ground for post-truth rhetors. Yet, this picture remains incomplete without factoring in the role of online platforms. We must continue the investigation of the structural transformation of the public sphere, delving into the dynamics of platform/surveillance capitalism, and particularly its mode of operation in social media.

The hybrid mediascape and the question of information supply

Critics from Aldous Huxley to Habermas and Postman were mainly worried about the reduction of the audience into a silent, passive recipient (Habermas 1991, 200–201). From this angle, the early enthusiasm about the internet and its potential for active engagement is understandable. Is it not preferable that people search for information independently, instead of just following the agenda set by the media? The development of the internet into a multimedia experience full of user generated content (known as Web 2.0) was greeted with an enthusiasm that likened it to a 'second Gutenberg event' that would radically democratise politics. Perhaps bathing in the naivete of liberal democracy's triumphs after the fall of the Berlin Wall, it was assumed (by some, at least) that the forces of free markets and civil society would always produce pro-democracy results.

The first step on the road to understanding why this has not been the case is recognising that social media functions as a part of a technological environment defined by a superabundance of information. The question is not merely one of substance (what information is available) – it is a matter of how we acquire information. The internet has replaced the television as the 'meta-medium' – the instrument that not only supplies us with information, but also directs our ways of knowing (Postman 2005, 78–79).

Psychological research suggests, for instance, that the instant availability of information online feeds our tendency to over-estimate our own understanding. The fast access to information blurs the boundary between internal ('in the head') and external ('in a book'), leading to inflated 'cognitive self-esteem'. In other words, we think we know much more than we actually do (Fisher et al. 2015). Often, the result resembles the image presented by Adorno and Horkheimer in 1944 (2007, xvii), according to which 'the flood of precise information and brand-new amusements make people smarter and more stupid at once'.

This has been vividly illuminated by the 'infodemic' that accompanied the Covid-19 pandemic. Traditionally, one of the major challenges for making sense of crisis situations has been the paucity of available information. To some extent, this still holds true for element of the Covid-19 pandemic. Arguably, however, for the meaning-making processes during the crisis, the main challenge for the populace has not been the absolute lack of information. It has been, instead, the ability to recognise the relevant, epistemologically sound, and politically utilisable knowledge from the flood of available information, misinformation, and disinformation. One manifestation of the disarray of information is the fact that disagreements are increasingly based on mutually contradictory bits of information first voiced by people claiming various degrees of expertise, and later amplified by political pundits and ordinary citizens. Hence, during the pandemic almost any decision or recommendation by public health authorities was vulnerable to criticism from a source, statistic, or expert pointing towards a different conclusion. Rather than fostering the democratic virtue of fallibilistic pluralism, public debate as a result becomes characterised by an aggressive need to 'be right' (see Lynch 2019; Arendt 1968, 28). In some cases, this buried any attempt to have a properly democratic debate – one where disagreement pertains to principled judgments, not to the possession of indisputable facts.

Social media platforms know that being buried under an unstructured flow of information is not an ideal user experience. As a solution, information the user encounters is typically filtered by algorithms. For O'Neil (2017), this can be compared to the editorial decisions of traditional media. But these decisions were clear and visible, being the same for everybody. Hence, they could form a shared ground for discussion. The 'newsfeeds' of social media, and the result pages of Google search, make similar 'editorial decisions' in a manner that is more individualised and less visible, hence evading the awareness of most users. This complicates the idea that the internet would enable liberation from an external agenda. If what individuals encounter in the newsfeed is algorithmically determined and personalised, even the members of the same political community can inhabit differently structured realities. We may then justifiably share the worry voiced by Sunstein (2018, 37–41) regarding the wilting of random encounters, shared experiences and somewhat overlapping conceptions of reality. During the impeachment hearings of President Trump, for example, the events appeared radically differently depending on whether they were followed via, say, CNN coverage or through a Facebook account whose 'likes' were exclusively on pro-Republican and pro-Trump pages.

Social media allows us to choose, or chooses for us, the sources of information in a way that buffs out the uncomfortable edges that facts tend to come with.

A scholarly consensus on the true scale of filter bubbles does not exist as yet, but polarisation and conflicting views on facts and reality are nevertheless an established fact (Marietta and Barker 2019). For example, on YouTube, where the recommendation algorithm steers around 70 percent of viewing time, the recommendations tend to bolster political biases and favour sensationalist videos – often highlighting conspiracist content or other forms of disinformation (Starr 2020, 80). Filter bubbles raise the risk of people being divided ever more clearly into their own mutually hostile cliques, equating the truth with their own group (Urbinati 2014, 4). Meanwhile, growing tribalism also implies that lying becomes increasingly acceptable from one's group, because it is seen as serving some higher end (Hendricks and Vestergaard 2018, 83; Rosenfeld 2018, 9). A manifestation of this that cuts through ideological divisions is the dominance of viral (often emotional) narratives weaved around first-person experiences. Such stories are all but immune to fact-checking due to their claim to representativeness that does not hinge on the factual accuracy of the particular story on which their appeal nevertheless rests (Mäkelä et al. 2021). Such divergence of experiences and reality conceptions erodes the basic respect between participants of a debate. No wonder that one characteristic phenomenon of social media is, in the words of Byung-Chul Han, a 'shitstorm' (Han 2017, 2–12).

The problems go beyond saying nasty things on the internet. Political theorists from Cicero to Rawls have alerted us to the potential threat of violence when disagreement relates primarily to truth (Urbinati 2014, 100). The events at Capitol Hill in 2021 proved this to be the case in the online era as well. However, the exact nature of polarisation – especially in the US – also attests to the link between the media and broader political trends. If it was merely a question of social media and algorithms, this would predict symmetrical polarisation of the media system. Notably, this is not the case. The US media ecosystem is characterised by asymmetric polarisation, where a niche has emerged on the right side of the political spectrum largely isolated from mainstream sources of news and strongly linked to various conspiracist agendas (Benkler 2020, 44–47). In the extreme, the information disorder allows for a strategy mastered by the likes of Steve Bannon and Roger Stone. For them, the point is no longer even upholding a certain political narrative by using lies, but rather emancipating politics from the horizon where adherence to facts is one vector in the critical evaluation of opinions and policies. This is done by disorienting the audience with a flood of stories and narratives, rather than sticking to only one. As Bannon famously described his strategy, the goal is to 'flood the zone with shit'. This exemplifies a strategic use of careless speech. The point is not to gain ground within the confines of a single policy issue as much as it is to eliminate the whole idea of a common world in the context of which political disagreements are played out according to the 'rules of the game'. While Bannon certainly draws from the playbook of older 'merchants of doubt' (for example, the tobacco and oil industries), the move from the traditional to social media has eliminated much of the viscosity introduced by professional journalists with editorial standards (Starr 2020, 69–70).

Of course, social media can also be used for truth-telling. Unlike some, I use the term rather strictly to refer to speech that can actually be said to be *truthful*. For example, the #MeToo and #BlackLivesMatter campaigns successfully used social media for raising public awareness about the structural injustices of contemporary society. In this sense, social media creates space for what Fraser (1990, 67) has called 'counterpublics'. By doing so, it also harbours the potential of restructuring the architecture of modern publics, i.e. challenging the historical exclusion of certain voices from democratic fora. Yet, the internet is also full of public and semi-public spaces used for the dissemination of disinformation and antidemocratic thinking. The period of the 2020 elections and the Capitol Hill riot in the US is the most flagrant example. Even after the most visible far-right 'Stop the Steal' group on Facebook was removed due to threats of violence, the movement continued to spread disinformation and plan the Capitol Hill riots across various Facebook pages. Through 2020, as the Tech Transparency Project (2021) summarises, 'Facebook's efforts to curb violent activity and disinformation were either too late or ineffective or both'. In less mainstream platforms, such as Parler, violent rhetoric and disinformation are even more prevalent, while generally reaching a smaller overall audience.

Blatant disinformation and violence are only one aspect of the phenomenon. Social media also serves as a platform for spaces dominated by hateful content – usually misogynist, racist, or homophobic in orientation and weaponised as a silencing tactic (Särmä 2020). The solution cannot lay merely in embracing the 'good' and rejecting the 'bad' when it comes to social media. Neither can we rely exclusively on individual-level interventions, media literacy programs or fact-checking. While important, these approaches remain ineffective if we do not grasp the bull by the horns, analysing the issue from the viewpoint of the imperatives of platform capitalism.

Welcome to the era of platform capitalism

To gauge the problem accurately, we must understand the operational logic of the online platforms. Platforms are 'digital infrastructures' that position themselves as intermediaries between two or more groups (Srnicek 2016,

42–43, 48). Most of these firms build their success on the extraction and refinement of data. This union of data and capital is widely considered a new type of economic formation and has been called surveillance capitalism or platform capitalism among other labels. The logic of the accumulation of surveillance capitalism relies on turning all spheres of human experience into quarries of data extraction – i.e. expropriating 'behavioural surplus', which is then refined into instruments of behavioural prediction and modification (Zuboff 2019, 8–9, 99, 200; Srnicek 2016, 39–40). While the general tendency is to expand this operation to everyday 'offline' life (e.g. through the Internet of Things), for our purposes it suffices to note that every aspect of 'the internet's computer-mediated architecture [...] is repurposed as an extraction architecture' (Zuboff 2019, 129). Key interfaces of this extraction architecture are user engagements – the main unit of the online attention economy, which includes clicks, views, viewing time, and shares (Hendricks and Vestergaard 2018, 1–17). Prioritisation of engagements as the pivots of data extraction leaves the door ajar for actors following the Bannon 'flooding' strategy. It also helps us understand why organised disinformation campaigns and bot armies are potentially so effective. Provocations, viral stories, and careless speech – i.e. statements indifferent to their truth-value and often blatantly disrespectful of democratic norms – are excellent sources of engagement, whereas facts and critical, pluralistic debate typically are not.

The platform companies have little interest in stemming the flood. On the contrary, since operations involving data become more profitable the more raw material you have, their business model relies on what Zuboff calls 'radical indifference'. In other words: 'it doesn't matter what is in the pipelines as long as they are full and flowing'. This acts as a constant invitation to, modifying Bannon's metaphor only a little, fill the pipes with shit – that is, with disinformation, conflicting narratives, and rage-inciting content. The chances are that – except for content considered disturbing almost universally, like child pornography – Facebook and other platforms will not interfere heavily with such content unless forced to do so by legislation. In fact, it seems likely that Facebook could turn down most mis-/disinformation on its site if it wanted to. This, however, would directly intervene with its logic of accumulation, which relies on the maximum amount of users sharing the maximum amount of content (Zuboff 2019, 509–12; Srnicek 2016, 45). Less content means less data, which means less capital and lower profits.

Towards an expanded notion of critical infrastructure

This chapter has sought to add to the understanding of post-truth politics by providing a critical genealogy of the digital public sphere. As the recourse to Habermas's notion of structural transformation suggests, having major parts of the architecture of public discourse in the hands of private ownership is not new in the context of modern history. The implications of private ownership for public discourse have always been ambivalent. Yet, it seems that the recent emergence of data-driven platform capitalism has introduced new threats that should be taken seriously. From the passive, sometimes mis- (or under-) informed citizens of the television era, we have moved to the polarised public of our hybrid era. Rather than reducing them to silence, the digital architecture of the contemporary public sphere invites citizens to consume disinformation, which has a high potential to inflame aggressive hyper-agitation either online or offline.

Thus far, legal regulation of the platforms has focused primarily on privacy concerns. As Zuboff's argument about surveillance demonstrates, privacy is indeed a key concern also politically. However, over-emphasising the role of the consumer over that of the citizen can also mean that regulative action fails to address some of the pressing threats to the public interest. What is needed is more focus on the role of the platforms as de facto public spaces – in other words, infrastructures of democracy. In addition to protecting privacy, we need to protect and take care of publicity. Security political discourse of the past two decades has been dominated by the notion of 'critical infrastructure'. Given that democracy is increasingly under attack globally, the factual basis of political decision-making should be considered a critical infrastructure in need of protection.

Caring for and protecting public discourse requires, among other things, a regulative framework that supports the diversity and plurality of online spaces and guarantees access to common sources of factual information (Dommett and Verovšek 2021). Pushing for such reforms is bound to incite resistance from the platform companies. They tend to consider 'old institutions like the law', to quote the Google CEO Larry Page, too viscous in principle to regulate digital technology. Any impediment to data extraction, in particular, is a direct threat to the platforms' logic of accumulation, and data extraction is best served by content that produces engagements (Zuboff 2019, 60, 104–105). Yet, as with other parts of critical infrastructure, regulation must be enacted to guarantee not only the factual basis of debate, but also the broader horizon of shared experiences – without which the facts and democracy itself lose their meaning.

References

Arendt, Hannah. 2006. *Between Past and Future: Eight Exercises in Political Thought*. London: Penguin.

Benkler, Yochai. 2020. 'A Political Economy of the Origins of Asymmetric Propaganda in American Media'. In *The Disinformation Age*, edited by W. Lance Bennett and Steven Livingston. Cambridge: Cambridge University Press.

Bennett, W.Lance and Steven Livingston, eds. 2020. *The Disinformation Age*. Cambridge: Cambridge University Press.

Dommett, Katharine, and Peter Verovšek. 2021. 'Promoting Democracy in the Digital Public Sphere: Applying Theoretical Ideals to Online Political Communication'. *Javnost – The Public.* Online First.

Fisher, Matthew, Mariel Goddu, and Frank Keil. 2015. 'Searching for Explanations: How the Internet Inflates Estimates of Internal Knowledge'. *Journal of Experimental Psychology: General* 144(3): 674–87.

Frankfurt, Harry. 2005. *On Bullshit*. Princeton: Princeton University Press.

Fraser, Nancy. 1990. 'Rethinking the Public Sphere: A Contribution to the Critique of Actually Existing Democracy'. *Social Text*, no. 25/26: 56–80.

Gesellschaft für deutsche Sprache. 2016. 'GfdS Wählt »postfaktisch« zum Wort Des Jahres 2016'. http://gfds.de/wort-des-jahres-2016/

Habermas, Jürgen. 1991. *The Structural Transformation of the Public Sphere: An Inquiry into a Category of Bourgeois Society*. Cambridge, MA: The MIT Press.

Han, Byung-Chul. 2017. *In the Swarm: Digital Prospects*. Cambridge, MA: The MIT Press.

Hendricks, Vincent and Mads Vestergaard. 2018. *Reality Lost: Markets of Attention, Misinformation and Manipulation*. New York: Springer.

Horkheimer, Max, and Theodor Adorno. 2007. *Dialectic of Enlightenment*. Stanford: Stanford University Press.

Hyvönen, Ari-Elmeri. 2018. 'Careless Speech: Conceptualizing Post-Truth Politics'. *New Perspectives* 26(3).

Kanno-Youngs, Zolan, and Cecilia Kang. 2021. '"They're Killing People":
Biden Denounces Social Media for Virus Disinformation'. *The New York
Times*, July 16, 2021, https://www.nytimes.com/2021/07/16/us/politics/
biden-facebook-social-media-covid.html

Lynch, Michael P. 2019. *Know-It-All Society: Truth and Arrogance in Political
Culture*. New York: Liveright.

Mäkelä, Maria, Samuli Björninen, Laura Karttunen, Matias Nurminen, Juha
Raipola, and Tytti Rantanen. 2021. 'Dangers of Narrative: A Critical Approach
to Narratives of Personal Experience in Contemporary Story Economy'.
Narrative 29(2): 139–59.

Marietta, Morgan, and David Barker. 2019. *One Nation, Two Realities:
Dueling Facts in American Democracy*. Oxford: Oxford University Press.

McIntyre, Lee. 2018. *Post-Truth*. Cambridge, MA: MIT Press.

O'Neil, Cathy. 2017. *Weapons of Math Destruction: How Big Data Increases
Inequality and Threatens Democracy*. New York: Crown.

Oxford Dictionaries. 2016. 'Word of the Year 2016 Is...'. https://en.
oxforddictionaries.com/word-of-the-year/word-of-the-year-2016

Postman, Neil. 2005. *Amusing Ourselves to Death: Public Discourse in the
Age of Show Business*. London: Penguin.

Rorty, Richard. 1981. *Philosophy and the Mirror of Nature*. Princeton:
Princeton University Press.

Rosenfeld, Sophia. 2018. *Democracy and Truth: A Short History*.
Philadelphia: University of Pennsylvania Press.

Särmä, Saara. 2020. 'Underbelly: Making Online Hate Visible'. *New
Perspectives* 28(1): 128–41.

Spicer, André. 2018. *Business Bullshit*. New York: Routledge.

Srnicek, Nick. 2016. *Platform Capitalism*. Cambridge: Polity.

Starr, Paul. 2020. "'he Flooded Zone: How We Became More Vulnerable to Disinformation in the Digital Era'. In *The Disinformation Age*, edited by W. Lance Bennett and Steven Livingston. Cambridge: Cambridge University Press.

Sunstein, Cass. 2018. *#Republic: Divided Democracy in the Age of Social Media*. Princeton: Princeton University Press.

Tanguay, Liane. 2019. 'Reality TV "Gets Real": Hypercommercialism and Post-Truth in CNN's Coverage of the 2016 Election Campaign'. In *Neoliberalism and the Media*, edited by Maria Meyers. New York: Routledge.

Tech Transparency Project. 2021. 'Capitol Attack Was Months in the Making on Facebook'. https://www.techtransparencyproject.org/articles/capitol-attack-was-months-making-facebook

Urbinati, Nadia. 2014. *Democracy Disfigured: Opinion, Truth, and the People*. Cambridge, MA: Harvard University Press.

Wischmeyer, Thomas. 2019. 'Making Social Media an Instrument of Democracy'. *European Law Journal* 25(2): 169–81.

Zuboff, Shoshana. 2019. *The Age of Surveillance Capitalism: The Fight for a Human Future at the New Frontier of Power*. New York: Public Affairs.

3

Trolling IR About Trolling in International Affairs

KYRIAKOS MIKELIS

'That's a troll!' Unless this statement is made while fishing or narrating a fairy or folk tale, it would likely be found when referring to either a provoking – possibly insulting – message or its conveyor. If a social or political scientist is merely asked to analyse trolls, then she would, in all probability, refer to neither fish, nor dwarfs nor giants but to someone being a provocateur or something disrupting in a communication, usually taking place on the internet and/or social media. The Merriam-Webster Dictionary addresses this meaning by defining 'to troll' as 'to antagonize (others) online by deliberately posting inflammatory, irrelevant or offensive comments or other disruptive content' or 'to harass, criticize, or antagonize (someone) especially by provocatively disparaging or mocking public statements, postings or acts' or 'to act as a troll'. Succinctly put, the phenomenon includes targeting, defaming and humiliating (Coleman 2014, 19). Even so, the meaning of trolls/trolling is fairly varied and not fixed, as is highlighted by the relevant scholarship, in respect to the acknowledgement of the term's initial appearance. Earlier manifestations seemed to predominantly refer more to humour or trickery than to merely offensiveness and harassment of individuals or of collective identities.

In this context, and addressing trolling with just a bit of a trolling spirit, this chapter constitutes an exercise in self-reflection and critical pedagogy, within the field/discipline of International Relations (IR). That is achieved by invoking the concept and its use, with the aim of contributing to the tackling of the post-truth predicament in world politics. On the one hand, the disruption of one's official narrative has increasingly become a challenging feature in a variety of arenas of social and political engagement. As shown below, those arenas include (dis)information, public diplomacy, cyberwar, communication and manipulation and lastly, identity, digital or social media politics.

Indicatively, trolls may well reflect socio-political and diplomatic antagonism. They may interfere in elections, affect political activism or be ultimately perceived as some sort of 'weapon'. At the very least, these aspects relate to the instrumental relevance of trolls in the conduct of global politics.

On the other hand, trolls may even compel scholars, students, citizens or collectivities to reflect upon the nature of politics and knowledge. Trolling thus becomes relevant in the discussion and problematisation of IR as a discipline, something that does not come out of the blue. Social science and particularly IR, even with some delay, have turned towards critical thinking about authority struggle and knowledge regulation. Notably, emphasis has been given on the very existence of an age of disruption and what the latter entails for IR and its critical interrogation, depicted as 'teaching International Relations in a time of disruption' (Smith and Hornsby, 2021).

In this regard, this chapter unravels the respective intricacies by discussing firstly the invocation of trolling in current global politics. Following this, the merits or challenges of a possible re-entry of the concept – in addressing this invocation within IR self-reflection – are discussed. In sum, the chapter is about what IR and the broader Social Sciences tell us about trolling and, respectively, what trolling may tell us about IR.

Trolling in international affairs

In the age of globalisation and a full-grown information society, a mere reference to the impact of social media on social or political affairs and cross-border communication is well anticipated. With all its intricacies, social media drives scholars to think on the dynamics and trajectory of the 'social' or of the 'political' (including the 'international') as well as on corresponding relations. Even diplomatic routines are subject to adjusting to the digital logic, illustrated by the growing employment of informal or humorous rhetoric as a resource of digital public diplomacy and nation-branding. The respective aims relate to attracting attention, agenda-setting, values projection and to the articulation of straightforward yet comprehensible diplomacy to broader audiences (Manor 2021, 61–64). Overall, digitally mediated communication is ideally characterised by Lemke and Habegger (2021: 239–244) as expansion (huge amounts of participants), acceleration (abundant information, immediacy) and divergence (polarisation, outrage culture, radicalisation, normalisation of trolling practices).

Attributing trolling as an essential characteristic of social media is subject to debate. Whether essential or not, the logic and practice of trolling are far from uncommon in the media, thus having a strong presence in socio-political affairs and communication. Mazarr et al. (2019) address this trait and trace 'the emerging risk of virtual societal warfare' as its major characteristic. Information-based aggression is asserted and it is subsequently considered to be the sum of a series of trends. These include the unfolding of large-scale social institutions with little accountability or trust, a diminishing faith in established institutions, the weakening of social capital, a rising polarisation pattern and the rise of populism. This aggression is further reflected in certain features. These are a trolling ethic, self-reinforcing echo chambers and the infosphere's fragmentation, along with the viral expansion of information within networked dynamics, general sensationalism, the concentration of information platforms, the role of influencers and lastly the immense growth of data collection. The first three features in particular are seen as principally differentiating the evolving situation compared to the past. As far as the trolling ethic is particularly concerned, it denotes the use of satirical memes, of inflated and fabricated stories or of merciless attacks. The purpose is to suspend dialogue, create trouble and strengthen argumentation. Therefore, it constitutes a viewpoint comprising irony, insolence and sensationalism aiming for humour, disruption or aggression (Mazarr et al. 2019, 14–21; 36–38).

Similarly, research in the politics of social media, with an emphasis on twitter and its role in international affairs, verifies the broader impact of technological shifts in temporality and functionality of communication. Furthermore, this specific case encompasses not only the logic of the latter (e.g. broadcasting and public diplomacy) or of low politics but also one of conflict and high politics. This is done by both representing and provoking emotions with a noticeable impact on the processes of conflict and on its (de)escalation. Trolling sharply reflects the links among wider shifts, the range of emotions and the power of social media. Transgressive behaviour is distinctively facilitated by the latter's structure, not least regarding Twitter, which intensifies individuals' or groups' proclivity for identity construction based on harassing and shaming (Duncombe 2019, 422–425).

Subsequently, this 'obvious' role of trolling as part of propaganda, disinformation, information manipulation or information warfare and indeed the very existence of what was termed '[Cyber] Troops, trolls and troublemakers' by Bradshaw and Howard (2017). The manipulation of social media, particularly in an organised fashion, involves an array of tactics: e.g., comment posting, individual targeting, government-sponsored sites/ applications or accounts, fake accounts, automation and content creation. Equally notable is the range of forms of participants such as government, politicians and parties, private contractors, volunteers and paid citizens (Bradshaw and Howard 2017, 8–17). In any case, it is important to note the growing articulation of troll groups with war-related terms and images, reflecting the portrayal of the internet – particularly on behalf of states – as a site of violence (Kamis and Thiel, 2015). References to troll farms, troll factories and troll industries are frequent enough – as is also the case with troll troops or troll armies.

An archetypical example, often quoted within the relevant literature, is the Russian-Ukrainian conflict – and it has included trolls from both sides. The Russian entity closely associated with the respective activities was eventually known as the Internet Research Agency (IRA). The equivalent Ukrainian entity is the Ukraine Information Army, founded by Ukraine's Ministry of Information Policy. Although there has certainly been no monopoly of state-sponsored trolling on behalf of a single country, the Internet Research Agency faced charges for interfering on various occasions, usually in electoral processes: e.g., in the US (2016), in Germany (2017) and the UK (2016). It was not just an issue of quantitative or of geographic expansion. A qualitative evolution has also been ascertained in terms of scope or targeting and sophistication. Specifically, there has been a rapid evolution beyond the framing of conflict, with an increasing aim of contributing to division, polarisation and uncertainty. In this respect, it would even make sense to target opposite groups, as long as there was message susceptibility. A major development that was also observed refers to tactics such as fake website making, local news outlet impersonation, micro-targeted campaigns and finally an increased robotisation or automatisation, i.e. bot activities and artificial intelligence with personalised and adaptive features (Pavlíková et al. 2021, 43–44; 54–58). The lines between trolling and diplomacy or other political means are often fine and unclear. This was seen in the case of the December 2016 'lame duck' tweet created by the Russian Embassy in London as a critique of US President Barack Obama who was nearing the end of his presidential term. Such humour employed by diplomats had a global impact and yet it faced critique for trolling (Manor 2021, 71–72).

According to research by Twitter, Internet Research Agency accounts with notable presence in the 2016 US presidential elections were found to be active also in the Brexit debate earlier that same year in the UK – essentially a form of repurposing. Moreover, the aim seemed to be making noise rather than exerting direct influence towards a specific direction. Finally, indications stood out for the existence of cyborg accounts, i.e., the addition of automated bot behaviour to human activity (Llewellyn et al. 2019, 1061; 1148). What may evidently rise here is the manipulation of public opinion in the digital sphere by means of coordinated campaigns, often in light of important political events. It is often state-sponsored, but not necessarily.

A comparison between trolls originating from specific countries (in this case, Russia and Iran) revealed a series of traits. In both examined cases, the respective campaigns were affected by the course of events, while behaviour (for example, the use of language) was not necessarily consistent over time, rendering detection complicated. Differences were discerned regarding ideology (for example, pro-Trump and anti-Trump) and the degree of influence and efficiency in respect to pushing URLs, whereby Russian trolls were particularly successful. The variance was also found with regards to the discussed topics depending on platforms and communities (Zannettou, et al., 2019, 353–354). This diversification is verified by a broader and global survey of organised manipulation by Bradshaw and Howard (2017). In fact, the latter relates to quite different countries. In authoritarian regimes, the process is often funded and coordinated by the government. In democratic states, it may also involve other entities such as political parties. Multiplicity might also characterise troll and cyber armies in respect to affiliation, funding and clientele which includes governments but also goes beyond them (Bradshaw and Howard 2017, 22–23). Furthermore, a similarly illustrative comparison of digital information warfare between a distinguished pair of countries hostile to each other (in this case, India and Pakistan) found the engagement of citizens of both states acting in a similar way. Human troll armies (rather than bots) posed as ordinary citizens. Most importantly, the plurality of contributors posted on hashtags of their corresponding state, without entering in counterarguments with the other side's contributors. The outcome was a favourable stance to the hashtags of one's own country, manifesting mentalities of jingoism and nationalism that served the policy choices of the respective governments (Hussain et al. 2021, 8–9).

Besides the impact of trolling in reflecting and exhibiting harsh bilateral or multilateral relations within the international arena – or its usual understanding in terms of propaganda – attention is also warranted towards domestic and cultural processes. For example, the case of Russia is cited as an example of a phenomenon called 'neutrollization' (industrialised trolling) – a process of a desecuritising nature whereby trolling is encouraged by the regime to preserve itself and to tackle civil society's perception of said regime as a societal security threat. Instead of obstructing the internet in an overtly authoritarian fashion, internet activism is used in such a way that the possibility of meaning is precluded via political disengagement and the breeding of doubt in a non-securitising manner. Here, there is a disruption not of an official viewpoint but of a context that could enable acts of securitisation against the regime (Kurowska and Reshetnikov 2018, 345–348). Another example refers to the emergence of political trolling through the lens of mediated populism. In this case, trolls are engaged in power networks and discourses which eventually help the establishment consolidate power within the respective country. Trolls are essentially used by the state and government to enforce citizen mobilisation in certain pathways. It may reflect features of populism, like the adoration of people and the demonisation of outsiders – or even a culture of lynching and censorship and attacking non-government-friendly individuals (Bulut and Yörük 2017, 4093–4095).

In the aforementioned cases, trolls 'bite' or fight on behalf of the government or regime. However, trolls may 'bite' or fight back or against established structures of power. A notable example of this is the case of the movement known as Anonymous – since it reflects the potential and limits of trolling. In its initial appearance, the movement was seen, fairly justifiably, as just another form of trolling. Yet, it turned out to be a politically motivated insurgency that cannot be reduced to its undisputable trolling roots. This feature has been presented in terms of a 'metamorphosis from trolling misfits to the misfits of activism' (Coleman 2014, 8) or a shift 'away from ungovernable trolling pandemonium to engage in the global political sphere' (Coleman 2014, 3). Trolling's global reach and wide range are reflected not just in phenomena like Anonymous but also in global trolling. An example relates to the inauguration speech of Donald Trump in January 2017. Trolling attitudes related to provocation, repetition and satire or even a pseudo-sincere stance. These were exhibited regardless of country of origin – thus transcending national lines. Then again, the cultural dimension makes some difference, with the example of respective instances originating more from individualistic countries rather than collectivist ones (Fichman 2020, 13–14).

Overall, the instrumental relevance of trolls comes up as pertinent in a variety of aspects: interstate antagonism, exerting influence in major events, and state-sponsored (or not) activism. In a discourse characterised by the heavy presence of information warfare, the weaponisation of trolls seems nearly inevitable.

The problematisation of IR through trolling

The above narration addresses trolling as a phenomenon with multiple dimensions and manifestations. In the end, though, it gets down to the conceptualisation of trolls in terms of weaponisation, i.e. the use of trolls in manipulation and confrontation within interstate relations or in favour of a certain power structure – usually (though not always) a state. Interestingly, the employment of the war metaphor on behalf of states in the analysis of cyberspace and the internet was once perceived as trolling itself – insofar as it was presumably contributing to a shift in the respective discourse (Kamis and Thiel 2015, 2). There is validity in this claim as the aforementioned metaphor helps states to preserve their role. Regardless of the metaphor's actual origins, though, this employment has essentially become the norm, if it was ever the exception. One need not say that there is something wrong per se with this neatness, the state-centric highjack of trolls and power-focus.

Since, however, trolling has much to do with disruption, it is intriguing to reflect upon how the former may serve to disrupt the field/discipline of IR and another key practice, apart from war – diplomacy.

First, a brief note on reflection is necessary. The literature on IR identity, which extensively manifests reflective or critical concerns, has been dubbed as 'reflexive studies on IR' by Grenier (2015). Schematically, it includes three perspectives. A geo-epistemic dimension relates to the hierarchy-oriented inquiry of the field's evolution at multiple geographical settings. A historiographical dimension refers to the unravelling of dominant and of dissident or alternative narratives concerning the field's history and, eventually, story or identity. Finally, the sociological perspective includes the exploration of the patterns of communication and the power relations in knowledge production (Grenier 2015, 74–76). Whether in philosophical, historical or sociological terms, disciplinary identity is at the epicentre regarding content, context, features and the practice of IR. In fact, there has been no shortage of voices that assert or request the death or end of 'IR', as we 'know' it, and its 'theory' (see Sjoberg 2017, 167–8), usually meaning its Westphalian straightjacket.

Problematisation within IR is enhanced in light of the trolling phenomenon. It is exemplified in the relation of the latter to diplomacy – a core feature of IR-related practice. Compared to the image of conflict or of war, and its incorporation of trolling as already shown above, there has hardly been an equivalent success as regards to the diplomatic practice of hijacking trolls. Evidently, 'diplomacy itself is not immune to trolling' (Duncombe 2019, 423). It is considered not only scarcely compatible with the latter, but also threatened by it. Pessimism and scepticism for the prospects of digital diplomacy rise. They are based on the divergence in structures and logic, i.e. traditional diplomacy's formalisation and consensus-orientation versus the openness or looseness of social media (Lemke and Habegger 2021, 231). In this sense, states and international organisations face a predicament: 'to be a diplomat or to be a troll, that is the question before us' (Lemke and Habegger 2021, 260). Drenzer (2015) expressed a more pragmatic view that trolling presumably constitutes an option adopted by statesmen and by officials or a part of great power rivalry as well as a sign for a possible shift of diplomatic norms. What seemed as undiplomatic would rapidly become part of diplomatic and political exchange. This emergence of diplo-trolling was enabled by the difficulty in avoiding a dispute, especially in instigations by prominent politicians or diplomats. Despite the small space for meaningful dialogue, negotiation is possible but not without the toll of troll, namely increased costs and the interpretation of failed communication as a lack of international respect.

Concerning the game-changing potential of diplo-trolling, it eventually seems to follow the general trend of communication technology's impact on global affairs. Three phases appear concerning optimism, disillusionment and lastly realism, i.e. acceptance of both hopeful trajectories and troubling facets (Drezner 2015). So, Drezner seems to answer affirmatively, if cautiously, to the provocative question: 'it is diplo-trolling, but is it diplomacy after all?'. However, the key issue is how this question arises from the respective discussion – constituting a disruptive reflection on the nature of diplomacy and showing that, in light of trolling practices, the conduct or conceptualisation of diplomacy is not so neat. Trolling doesn't replace diplomacy or make it disappear. But along with the replication of the confrontational logic, it sets the ground for attempts at (re)considerations of diplomacy.

The aforementioned disruptive reflection does not limit itself to the subject matter of IR. It is also applicable to its (meta)theory. Beier (2021) highlights this by presenting the field's history in a non-neat fashion, particularly in terms of a discordant mixture of voices and stories – which allows for the critical engagement of students and for the appraisal of problematising and defamiliarising accounts, particularly those of a commonsensical nature. The challenge of internet trolls and alternative facts to the shifting boundaries of political imagination cannot but be noticed, raising worry about indeterminate knowledge claims. Similarly, fake news evidently challenges established ways of teaching. However, it is a different issue whether a 'stable truth' perspective is the solution to addressing the respective problem, when taking into account that it often leads to overlooking the regulatory practices for the production or the validation of knowledge (Beier 2021, 64–67).

At the same time, the critical lenses towards disruption, related to conspiratorial discourse or fake news and post-truth, seemingly invite the very disruption of the right for freedom of expression. This postulation does not mean the denial of that right. Yet, it is a reminder that such a rights claim should be uttered in connection with responsibility instead of merely defying it. The acknowledgment of disruption as a right or even as a duty, on behalf of scholarship and a critical perspective, necessitates critique against disruption of responsibility, i.e. against the process of equating ideas with opinion and rendering the latter as valid on the basis of the right for its existence. Thus, a collegial ethos involving the mutual and common responsibility of those who engage in knowledge practices serves as an important criterion. In this rationale, it is not an issue of juxtaposing 'good' or 'bad' knowledge claims but an issue of knowledge as a social practice as well as of the unfolding of the power of expertise, along with the politics of knowledge authority. Subsequently, criticising the weaponisation of fake news or trolls (especially when refusing or silencing dissident viewpoints) needs to be complemented by the awareness of the possibility for reification of knowledge claims. From the point of view of critical pedagogy and the decolonisation of scholarly knowledge production, disruptive thought and practice (with a range from conspiracy theories to trolling) can even be addressed as a thinking mode that contributes to the problematisation of authority – or of power – as well as to the enhancement of critical potential and of political imagination. However, this is the case only as long as the criterion of responsibility in knowledge practices is fulfilled (Beier 2021, 70–72).

The aforementioned vision falls within critical pedagogy which emphasises the varied role of disruption, namely: 'teaching as disruption', 'disrupting the discipline through teaching' and 'disruptions to teaching IR' – the broad aim here is to transcend the IR mainstream (Smith and Hornsby 2021, 3–5). Furthermore, it is compatible with the call for 'undisciplined IR', meaning IR characterised by 'thinking without a net' (Sjoberg, 2017). The logic of trolling here is latently present in one of the features of such an IR undiscipline, namely the very notion of the undisciplined. The latter is synonymous with terms such as unruly, disorderly and disruptive – appraising the absence of demands for methodological compliance or for political correctness or rules within the state and academic institutions. Like the aforementioned vision, a criterion for the disruptive practice is deemed crucial, namely the existence of purpose. Facets of undisciplined IR also include the following. Firstly: a non-orthodox stance towards epistemology, particularly appraising incoherence, a rogue mentality and the rejection of knowledge accumulation. Secondly: a purposefully unruly conduct. Thirdly: the pluralist search for approximation of knowledge, e.g. in terms of gratification, justice or rebellion. Finally: the perception of knowledge accumulation as misguided and hollow (ibid., 161–163). Certainly, the celebration of trolling here is not an appraisal of internet trolls who fight with each other and reproduce power relations. Instead, it emerges as a means for the contestation of academic hierarchies and dominant patterns.

Evidently, there are affinities of the above rationale with the emphasis, from a critical standpoint, on the possibility for trolling rising within cultural politics in a counter-hegemonic fashion as a way of struggling against dominant ideological frameworks. This may be done in cases of subversive affirmation on behalf of trolls who mock hegemonic discourse, performing the transgression of the limits of identities by means of not only humour but also over-identification. Indeed, a relevant option on behalf of a troll is to conceal themselves as the 'other', in order to forge a counter-identity against a prevalent discourse. This predicament doesn't negate the quite often reactionary manifestations of trolling and it doesn't equate all threats to normalcy with each other. However, awareness is raised on the emergence of trolling as a cultural feat that affects political ideologies. Transgressive passions are awakened, bringing up emotions and subsequently (dis) empowering identification (Mylonas and Kompatsiaris 2021, 35–36).

Overall, there is some margin for trolling as a method of critical inquiry and contestation. But this occurs only through the fulfilment of certain criteria. Taking into account the variety of aggression and transgression's forms and motives with a range including randomness, revolutionary mood, specific symbolic frameworks, justice or just 'the lulz' – 'a spirited but often malevolent brand of humour' (Coleman 2016, 4) – in such a critical process, a highly pertinent question is raised over 'what kind of trolling' emerges or 'whose trolling' occurs. The chapter's previous section ended with a reference to the inevitability of the weaponisation of trolls in the conduct of politics and international relations. In this section, a critical attempt of a discussion of trolling as a means against thought processes that privilege stability, reification or even the notion of inevitability was made. IR Scholars who want to present a not-so neat story of their discipline may adopt the spirit of trolling as a method, though with caveats like responsibility and purpose. In that way, there is no legitimisation of the trolling ethic on the internet, as discussed in the previous section.

Final Remarks

Overall, (international) politics is barely an exception to the general trend of manifold participation in trolling on behalf of multiple tight-knit groups, genres often assorted in respect to the target, political movements and even individuals. Succinctly put, it may well stem from either the ad hoc self-organisation of individuals or the collective orchestration in line with a regime agenda (Coleman 2014, 4, 19). This variety is the very reason for the difficulty and implausibility of presenting a neat story over trolling and IR in which trolling and its disruptive effects would either be absolutely condemned or unequivocally praised. It is the reason for the choice of naming this final section of the chapter 'final remarks' rather than naming it a conclusion. This choice serves as a reminder that the evaluation of the phenomenon and its effects relies on answering the 'whose trolling' predicament – that is, addressing its particular manifestations.

Subsequently, is a world of IR – which is increasingly characterised by troll(ing) – substantially different or even better? The analysis of trolling in international affairs entails what is here termed as 'instrumental relevance of trolls', with aspects such as manipulation, confrontation and antagonism which are further stressed by the notable use of the war metaphor. In this sense, trolling and its corresponding ethic, manifested in the digital sphere, seem to mark an IR trajectory in a business-as-usual mode. Despite trolling instances of resistance to power structures, the state-centric embracement or hijacking of trolling can hardly be missed, along with the 'disrupt the opponent/rival' mode. At the same time, this embracing is certainly not the end of the story when taking counter-hegemonic instances with a 'disrupt the system' mode into consideration. Those instances can be construed as pointing to a 'make troll, not IR' direction. And, they do not make up the whole of the story which does not emerge as neat. Given that the key concept here is disruption, this, probably, hardly comes as a surprise.

References

Beier, J. Marshall. 2021. "Traditions, Truths, and Trolls: Critical Pedagogies in the Era of Fake News." In *Teaching International Relations in a Time of Disruption*, 63–73. eds. Heather Smith, and David Hornsby. Palgrave Macmillan.

Bradshaw, Samantha, and Philip Howard. 2017. *Troops, Trolls and Troublemakers: A Global Inventory of Organized Social Media Manipulation*. Computational Propaganda Research Project. WP 2017.12.

Bulut, Ergin, and Erdem Yörük. 2017. "Digital Populism: Trolls and Political Polarization of Twitter in Turkey." *International Journal of Communication*, 11: 4093–4117.

Coleman, Gabriella. 2014. *Hacker, Hoaxer, Whistleblower, Spy. The Many Faces of Anonymous*. Verso.

Drezner, Daniel. 2015. "How Trolling Could Become the New International Language of Diplomacy." *Washington Post*, 15/5/2015.

Duncombe, Constance. 2019. "The Politics of Twitter: Emotions and the Power of Social Media. *International Political Sociology*." 13, 4: 409–429.

Fichman, Pnina. 2020. "The Role of Culture and Collective Intelligence in Online Global Trolling: The Case of Trolling Trump's Inauguration Speech." *Information, Communication & Society,* 1–16.

Grenier, Félix. 2015. "Explaining the Development of International Relations: The Geo-epistemic, Historiographical, Sociological Perspectives in Reflexive Studies on IR." *European Review of International Studies* 2, 1: 72–89.

Hussain, Shabir, Farrukh Shahzad, and Adam Saud. 2021. "Analyzing the State of Digital Information Warfare Between India and Pakistan on Twittersphere." *SAGE Open* (July-September 2021): 1–11.

Kamis, Ben, and Thorsten Thiel. 2015. *The Original Battle Trolls: How States Represent the Internet as a Violent Place*. PRIF/HSFK, WP 23.

Kurowska, Xymena, and Anatoly Reshetnikov. 2018. "Neutrollization: Industrialized Trolling as a pro-Kremlin Strategy of Descuritization." *Security Dialogue* 49, 5, 345–363.

Lemke, Tobias, and Michael Habegger. 2021. "Diplomat or Troll? The Case Against Digital Diplomacy." In *Digital Diplomacy and International Organizations. Autonomy, Legitimacy and Contestation*, 229–266. eds. Corneliu Bjola, and Ruben Zaiotti. Routledge.

Llewellyn, Clare, et al. 2019. "For Whom the Bell Trolls: Shifting Troll Behaviour in the Twitter Brexit Debate." *Journal of Common Market Studies*, 57, 5: 1148–1164.

Manor, Ilan 2021. "The Russians are Laughing! The Russians are Laughing! How Russian Diplomats Employ Humour in Online Public Diplomacy." *Global Society* 35, 1: 61–83.

Mazarr, Michael et al. 2019. *The Emerging Risk of Virtual Societal Warfare: Social Manipulation in a Changing Information Environment*. RAND.

Mylonas, Yiannis, and Panos Kompatsiaris. 2021. "Trolling as Transgression: Subversive Affirmations Against Neoliberal Austerity." *International Journal of Cultural Studies* 24, 1: 34–55.

Pavlíková, Miroslava, Barbora Šenkýřová, and Jakub Drmola. 2021. "Propaganda and Disinformation Go Online." In *Challenging Online Propaganda and Disinformation in the 21st Century*. 43–74. eds. Miloš Gregor and Petra Mlejnková. Palgrave Macmillan.

Sjoberg, Laura. 2017. "Undisciplined IR. Thinking Without a Net." In *What's the Point of International Relations?*. 159–169. eds. Synne Dyvik, Jan Selby, and Rorden Wilkinson. London and New York: Routledge.

Smith, Heather, and David Hornsby. 2021. "Introduction: Teaching International Relations in a Time of Disruption and Pandemic." In *Teaching International Relations in a Time of Disruption*. 1–7. eds. Heather Smith, and David Hornsby. Palgrave Macmillan.

Zannettou, Savvas et al. 2019. "Who Let The Trolls Out? Towards Understanding State-Sponsored Trolls." WebSci '19 (June 30–July 3): 353–362.

4

US Foreign Wars, Mass Marketing, and the Development of Post-Truth Politics

IDO OREN

Since 2016, when the Oxford English Dictionary selected post-truth as its Word of the Year, it has become commonplace to assert that we have entered an era of post-truth politics. In this chapter, I argue that, although the term post-truth may be relatively new, the social and political culture that the term denotes – a culture in which public opinion is not shaped by fact-based arguments so much as by reality-creating chanting of talking points – has been evolving for at least a century, if not longer. What may be new about the present is not that we have entered a new era characterised by the repeated assertion of talking points so much as that post-truth has itself become one of the talking points that saturate our discourse. Furthermore, I argue that the evolution of this post-factual culture has been pivotally shaped by the domestic politics of US foreign wars, most notably the campaigns to sell to the American public the US interventions in Europe in 1917 and Iraq in 2003.

I first sketch the propaganda campaign orchestrated by the Wilson Administration in 1917–1918 to rally support for the war effort. Public chanting of anti-German talking points was an integral part of the campaign. I then discuss how wartime propaganda methods were later transplanted to the realm of mass marketing. Commercial and political advertising campaigns have come to consist not in communicating facts about products or political candidates so much as in constant repetition of logos and taglines. When such campaigns succeed, they perform speech acts, that is, their taglines become the product (or candidate) they ostensibly refer to. Finally, I explain how such marketing practices returned with a vengeance to the foreign policy sphere in the Bush administration's campaign to mobilise public support for the 2003 invasion of Iraq. The campaign's central tagline was Iraqi 'weapons of mass destruction'. This ambiguous phrase – chanted by the administration and echoed by a chorus of journalists, commentators, and the public at large – became the Iraqi threat it ostensibly referred to.

First World War propaganda and the birth of post-truth culture

If there is a historical moment that can be plausibly said to mark the birth of post-truth culture, it was the moment in which – a century before post-truth would become Word of the Year – the United States, led by President Woodrow Wilson, swung from neutrality to all-out intervention in the First World War. In November 1916 Wilson was re-elected on the strength of a campaign whose primary mantra was 'He Kept Us Out of the War' (Kennedy 2004, 12). But just a few months later, the very man who 'owed his victory' to this slogan, reversed his policy of neutrality 180 degrees (Kennedy 2004, 12). In a famous address on 2 April 1917, Wilson implored the US Congress to declare war on Germany, intoning another memorable talking point: 'The World Must Be Made Safe for Democracy' (Kennedy 2004, 42).

Wilson was understandably worried that the American people would not rally behind the war effort. After all, the cause of neutrality was highly popular, or else he might not have won re-election by intoning that he kept America out of the war. Moreover, millions of Americans – including ethnic Germans, Irish, and Jews – sympathised with the German side and/or harboured intense antipathy toward Britain and Russia, America's newfound allies. Against this backdrop, and in the absence of a clear and present danger to the US homeland, 'the Wilson administration was compelled to cultivate – even to manufacture – public opinion favourable to the war effort' (Kennedy 2004, 46)

The administration thus launched a massive propaganda campaign – led by a new federal agency called the Committee on Public Information (CPI) – to sell the war to the American people. The CPI used newspapers, magazines, posters, radio, and movies to spark patriotic emotions and drum up enthusiasm for the war. Additionally, the CPI sponsored and trained 75,000 'Four-Minute Men' who made millions of short speeches around the country in support of the war effort. These speakers did not make rational arguments that appealed to the intellect of their listeners – it is virtually impossible to present a persuasive argument supported by detailed evidence in four minutes. What the speakers rather did was to repeatedly chant talking points and key phrases. For example, repeating the terms 'democracy' and 'liberty' in association with the United States while repeating words like 'beast' and 'atrocity' in association with the German enemy. As historian David Kennedy wrote, by early 1918 the CPI-guided short speeches became evocative of the 'Two Minutes Hate' exercises that George Orwell would describe in his novel *1984*. The CPI 'urged participatory "Four-Minute singing" to keep patriotism at "white heat"' (Kennedy 2004, 62).

From selling war to selling products and political candidates

The propaganda campaign orchestrated by the Wilson administration succeeded in generating public enthusiasm for the war effort. This gave some participants in the campaign the idea that the same techniques that proved so effective in selling the war to the American people could be used profitably to sell consumer products. Edward Bernays, a nephew of Sigmund Freud and a CPI propaganda operative, became convinced that 'if this could be used for war, it can be used for peace' (Rifkin 1991). Bernays enjoyed a long and successful career as one of America's leading experts in advertising, marketing, and public relations. He is often called the 'father of public relations' (Rifkin 1991).

The successful selling of US military intervention in Europe to a public that previously supported non-intervention was a pivotal event that ushered in the age of mass marketing, an age in which sellers of products were no longer content with providing facts about their products. In the mass consumer society that gradually took shape in the decades after World War I, the marketplace became characterised less by selling goods than by the aggressive marketing of brands, less by providing fact-based arguments about a product than by fostering emotional identification with values symbolised by brand names and icons/logos. For example, purchasers of Nike trainers do not only buy dependable athletic shoes, they also buy into values such as determination, dynamism, and cool (Johnson 2012, 3). Arguably the principal characteristic of modern mass marketing campaigns – a characteristic 'so obvious' that its significance is 'sometimes neglected' (Cook 1992, 227) – is repetition. Repetition, repetition, repetition.

Advertisers bombard us with symbols such as brand logos (the Nike swoosh), icons (Marlboro Man; Mr. Clean), and taglines ('Just do it'; 'Intel Inside'). These are repeated over and over with the aim that they would become etched in our minds like earworms – catchy tunes that involuntarily and repetitively play in our heads. As the political and corporate consultant Frank Luntz explained in his book *Words that Work*, the marketing messages that become stuck in our heads are typically brief and simple. Effective advertisers do not use a sentence when a phrase will do, and they use abbreviations whenever possible: 'the most unforgettable catchphrases ... contain only single- or at the most two-syllable words. And when they initially haven't been so simple, someone has stepped in to shorten them'. Thus, the Macintosh computer became Mac. Similarly, Federal Express, Kentucky Fried Chicken, and British Petroleum abbreviated their official names to FedEx, KFC, and BP (Luntz 2007, 6–7). The point is not that marketing campaigns never misfire – the history of advertising is rife with failures. But of those campaigns that succeed, perhaps their most remarkable feature is that the verbal and visual symbols spouted by the marketers unite with the brand being marketed. As Luntz put it, 'The most successful taglines are not seen as slogans for a product. They *are* the product' (Luntz 2007, 98; emphasis original). Similarly, enduring corporate icons such as the Marlboro Man and the Energizer Bunny 'aren't shills trying to *talk* us into buying' a pack of cigarettes or a package of batteries. 'Just like the most celebrated slogans, they *are* the products' (Luntz 2007, 100; emphases original). Although Luntz is a practical man, not a philosopher, his argument can readily be translated into the idiom of the philosophy of language. Luntz basically says that the verbal symbols repeatedly uttered by advertisers sometimes perform successful *illocutionary speech acts* (Austin and Urmson 2009). In other words, these phrases become the things they ostensibly refer to. They create reality rather than merely describe a pre-existing factual reality.

As mass marketing and advertising techniques became ubiquitous in the commercial marketplace, they increasingly migrated to other social spheres. As French philosopher Francois Baudrillard wrote in 1981, 'All current modes of activity tend toward ... the *form* of advertising, that of a simplified operational mode, vaguely seductive, vaguely consensual' (Baudrillard 1994, 87; emphasis original). Baudrillard further observed that politics absorbed the operational mode of advertising more fully than other spheres. In contemporary society, 'there is no longer any difference between the economic and the political, because the same language reigns in both' (Baudrillard 1994, 88). Returning now from the French philosopher to the American practitioner, Luntz wrote almost as if Baudrillard were guiding his hand: 'It's hard to tell who is in greater demand today: the Madison Avenue branding experts who are brought in to teach political parties how to define themselves, or the political consultants brought into corporate boardrooms to teach businesses how to communicate more effectively'. Madison Avenue techniques, Luntz added, 'firmly took hold in Washington during the Reagan years – and they continue to drive our politics today' (Luntz 2007, 72).

Luntz may have been too cautious in dating the marriage of Madison Avenue and Washington to the Reagan years. In fact, as US presidency scholar Samuel Popkin noted, 'Working to develop a brand name ... has always been part and parcel of preparing for a run at higher offices' (Popkin 2012, 23). And since at least 1952, when an infectious tagline written by a marketing executive – 'I like Ike' – powered Dwight Eisenhower to the presidency (Peterson 2009, 66), the branding strategies of US presidential candidates have prominently included the spouting forth of catchphrases: 'It's morning again in America' (Reagan, 1984); 'It's the economy, stupid' (Clinton, 1992); 'Yes, we can!' (Obama, 2008); 'Make America great again' (Trump, 2016). Indeed, inasmuch as his last name was a recognisable brand long before Donald Trump entered politics, his 2016 presidential campaign took the unification of name and product (political candidate) to a new level.

To recapitulate my argument so far, a central feature of post-truth culture – the repetition of talking points that do not merely describe a factual reality but create reality – has been part of American social, economic, and political life for many decades. The shaping of reality through repetitive spouting of words and symbols is not confined to domestic affairs. In fact, the origins of what is now called 'post-truth politics' go back to the campaign to sell America's intervention in World War I to the American people.

Back to selling war, in Iraq: WMD, WMD, WMD

In the remainder of this chapter, drawing on Oren and Solomon (2013; 2015), I return to US foreign relations and focus on a more recent case in which a government-orchestrated propaganda campaign successfully drummed-up enthusiasm for a war. I consciously use 'drum-up' because this campaign was metaphorically tantamount to the rhythmic beating of war drums. The campaign succeeded not by providing the American people with a fact-based argument about a foreign threat, which the public in turn considered rationally and found persuasive. It rather succeeded by continually repeating a catchphrase (or talking point) and by virtue of the incessant repetition of the catchphrase by the media and the public at large, which created a metaphorical drumbeat, or a choral chant: weapons of mass destruction, weapons of mass destruction, weapons of mass destruction, WMD, WMD, WMD. The choral incantation of the phrase performed an illocutionary speech act, that is, it did not merely describe a threat so much as it created and shaped a reality of a grave, existential danger.

In the aftermath of 11 September 2001, even though the mastermind of the attacks was based in Afghanistan, the George W. Bush administration began depicting Iraq as a grave menace to US and world security. During the run-up to the March 2003 invasion, the central theme of the administration's case against Iraq was the danger of Iraqi 'weapons of mass destruction'. Beginning with the January 2002 State of the Union address, Bush and senior administration officials uttered this phrase multiple times in most of their public appearances.

In August 2002 the White House was put on the defensive by a growing opposition galvanised by an opinion article in the *Wall Street Journal*. Titled 'Don't Bomb Saddam', the article was authored by former National Security Advisor Brent Scowcroft, a confidante of the president's father. To regain momentum, the White House Chief of Staff, Andrew Card, convened a high-level group whose mission was to market a war in Iraq. Although the formation of this group – the White House Iraq Group (WHIG) – was not made public, Card hinted at its task on 6 September 2002, when he told the *New York Times* that 'From a marketing point of view, you don't introduce new products in August'. Among the members of the WHIG were several specialists in strategic communication, including the president's senior political advisor, Karl Rove. In candid comments quoted by *New York Times* writer Ron Suskind in late 2004, Rove said that that journalists like Suskind lived 'in what we call the reality-based community', which Rove defined as 'people who "believe that solutions emerge from your judicious study of discernible reality"'. Rove added that the world does not work like this anymore:

> We're an empire now, and when we act, we create our own reality. And while you're studying that reality – judiciously, as you will – we'll act again, creating other new realities, which you can study too, and that's how things will sort out. We're history's actors ... and you, all of you, will be left to just study what we do (Suskind 2004).

Whether or not he ever studied the philosophy of language, Rove's comment sounded like he had a solid grasp of the concept of speech act.

The WHIG coordinated a dramatic public relations offensive to sell the war to the American public. With the launching of this campaign, the use of the talking point 'weapons of mass destruction' by administration officials increased markedly. In an appearance on CNN on the campaign's first day – 8 September 2002 – National Security Advisor Condoleezza Rice uttered the phrase 13 times. In a televised prime-time speech in Cincinnati a month later, Bush alluded to 'weapons of mass destruction' eight times in 26 minutes. On 3 January 2003, speaking to troops in Fort Hood, Texas, Bush said:

> The Iraqi regime has used weapons of mass destruction. They not only had weapons of mass destruction, they used weapons of mass destruction. They used weapons of mass destruction in other countries, they have used weapons of mass destruction on their own people. That's why I say Iraq is a threat, a real threat.

The persistent repetition of the phrase 'weapons of mass destruction' was, therefore, a central aspect of the Bush administration's campaign to sell the Iraq war to the American people. Senator Lincoln Chafee of Rhode Island, the only Republican senator who opposed the war, was hardly exaggerating when he later complained that the administration's case for invading Iraq consisted in a 'steady drumbeat of weapons of mass destruction, weapons of mass destruction, weapons of mass destruction'.

To become unified with the threat that it ostensibly referred to, it was not enough for the phrase to be repeated by the administration. To effectively create a menacing reality, this phrase had to be accepted and adopted by its audience – the media and the public at large. And indeed, before too long, 'weapons of mass destruction' became a daily staple of the American press. As Figure 4.1 shows, the frequency with which the *Wall Street Journal* printed this phrase was virtually zero in the 1980s and moderate in the 1990s before spiking dramatically in 2002 and 2003. A similar pattern was characteristic of other leading newspapers. And, as illustrated by figure 4.2, during the twelve months preceding the invasion of Iraq in March 2003 the incidence of 'weapons of mass destruction' in leading US publications has increased almost tenfold. Much of this increase coincided with the launching of the government's marketing campaign in early September 2002. No sooner than it flooded the US media, the phrase 'weapons of mass destruction' invaded the everyday talk of ordinary Americans at work, at home, and so on. This linguistic invasion was evidenced by the fact that the American Dialect Society selected the phrase as its 2002 'Word of the Year', that is, the year's most 'newly prominent or notable' vocabulary item.

As noted earlier, in commercial marketing, some of the most memorable brand names are abbreviations: CNN; KFC, FedEx. And, just as these corporations have profited from the abridgment of their names, so has the marketing of the Iraq war benefitted from the abbreviation of the flabby 'weapons of mass destruction' into a trim acronym, WMD. Whereas the acronym WMD almost never appeared in America's major newspapers in the 1990s, during the lead-up to the Iraq War the same newspapers printed this abbreviation hundreds of times. As the war approached, the acronym became so commonplace that reporters and commentators no longer felt compelled to spell it out (that is, they increasingly referred to WMD in the same manner that they routinely refer to, say, CNN without spelling out Cable News Network). The drumbeat echoed by the media became peppier: WMD, WMD, WMD.

In an insightful 'note on abridgment', Marcuse wrote that, even as abbreviations perform a perfectly reasonable function of simplifying speech – it is simpler to say NATO than North Atlantic Treaty Organization – they also perform an inconspicuous rhetorical function: 'help[ing] to repress undesired questions'. For example,

> NATO does not suggest what North Atlantic Treaty Organization says, namely a treaty among the nations on the North Atlantic – in which case one might ask questions about the membership of Greece and Turkey (Marcuse 1991, 94).

In keeping with Marcuse's analysis, the popularisation of WMD helped 'repress undesired questions' surrounding administration statements such as (in President Bush's words) 'They used weapons of mass destruction in other countries, they have used weapons of mass destruction on their own people'. Because WMD elides the words 'mass destruction', the growing prominence of the abbreviation in public discourse made it less likely that people would stop their chanting to ask questions like: can poison gas – the weapon that the above statement interchanged 'weapons of mass destruction' for – truly cause 'mass destruction' even as gas cannot destroy property? Did the gas the Iraqi regime use against 'its own people' really cause 'mass destruction'? Could the employment of chemical weapons by Iraq truly pose a grave danger to the security of the United States? In sum, the incantation of abbreviations like WMD perform the rhetorical function of taking us even further away from concrete factual reality than the chanting of the full phrase.

Abbreviation aside, some readers may wonder: Isn't 'weapons of mass destruction' a clear and unproblematic reference to alleged 'facts on the ground' in Iraq? Can't we simply check the facts and determine whether it was true that Iraq possessed weapons of mass destruction? Indeed, this was precisely how the US public debate was framed in the war's aftermath: did Iraq truly possess these weapons? If not, did the Bush administration lie to the American people (and the world) or merely suffer an unintentional intelligence failure? But I want to suggest that checking facts about weapons of mass destruction is not so simple because, like other common terms in US foreign policy discourse, this phrase is ambiguous and has multiple meanings. What exactly is meant by rogue state? Axis of evil? Ethnic cleansing? Soft/smart power? The meaning of such terms, like that of 'weapons of mass destruction', is more equivocal and historically variable than one might think. They are, in other words, empty signifiers.

When the term 'weapons of mass destruction' first appeared in diplomatic documents and in the US press in November 1945, it had no clear definition. In subsequent arms control negotiations held at the United Nations, diplomats and commentators debated a wide range of definitions before the UN Commission on Conventional Armament resolved in 1948 that 'weapons of mass destruction' included atomic, radiological, biological, and chemical weapons, as well as future weapons capable of comparable destruction. During the Cold War, however, the phrase receded from public view and, on the rare occasions it was mentioned in the US press, it was typically associated with nuclear weapons alone. The phrase 'weapons of mass destruction' was entirely absent from media reporting on instances in which chemical agents were undoubtedly used in warfare, including the widespread use of riot control agents and herbicides by the United States in Vietnam. Nor was the phrase mentioned in US press reporting on the use of poison gas by the Egyptian air force in Yemen, which resulted in hundreds of civilian deaths. Most strikingly, in contrast with President Bush's statement in 2003 that 'The Iraqi regime has used weapons of mass destruction', this term was utterly omitted from US press reporting in the 1980s on Iraq's lethal chemical warfare against Iran and against its own Kurdish population.

In the 1990s, 'weapons of mass destruction' made a minor comeback into US foreign policy discourse because the phrase was incorporated into the 1991 UN Security Council resolution that set the terms of the Gulf War ceasefire and imposed an arms inspection regime on Iraq. At the same time, the phrase jumped from the realm of foreign relations to the text of a massive anticrime law passed by the US Congress. The Violent Crime Control and Law Enforcement Act of 1994 defined weapons of mass destruction in far broader terms than those of the UN's 1948 definition, including, for example, any conventional 'bomb, grenade, rocket having a propellant charge of more than four ounces'. Based on this legislation, federal prosecutors began pressing WMD charges regularly not only against terrorism suspects such as 'shoe bomber' Richard Reid but also in cases involving petty domestic crime. For instance, a short time after the US invaded Iraq to remove the existential threat of WMD, a man from Pennsylvania was sent to prison for mailing his former doctor a 'weapon of mass destruction' assembled from 'black gunpowder, a carbon dioxide cartridge, a nine-volt battery ... and dental floss'.

'Weapons of mass destruction', then, is an ambiguous figure of speech, an empty signifier. Throughout its history the meaning of the phrase has been contested and changeable. It has had multiple meanings and it has meant different things to different people. Furthermore, even if foreign policy experts may have had a clear idea in their minds of what the term meant, the fact remains that before the Bush administration started intoning this term in 2002, most Americans have either never heard it or, if they have, they did not share a clear concept of what it precisely meant.

Here, I want to make an important point. As older readers may recall, the Iraq War was a divisive issue in American politics and a sizable minority of Americans adamantly opposed the invasion. Yet the chanting of WMD, WMD, WMD, transcended the political divide because opponents of the war, too, embraced the term, repeating it reflexively and uncritically. For example, speaking on the same CNN program in which Condoleezza Rice kicked off the campaign to sell the Iraq war to the American people, Senator Bob Graham – a Democrat from Florida who would later vote against authorising the war – uttered 'weapons of mass destruction' seven times.

By joining the chorus chanting 'WMD', the opponents of the war helped consolidate a generalised atmosphere of danger even as they were not persuaded by the Bush administration's case for war. When Americans were asked by pollsters whether they supported or opposed the use of force against Iraq, the results were exceptionally stable over time. In survey after survey conducted throughout 2002 and early 2003, just under sixty percent of the respondents expressed support for an invasion while just over a third of them indicated opposition. Remarkably, the launching of the administration's war marketing campaign in September 2002 made virtually no dent in this pattern. There is little evidence, then, that the administration persuaded the American people to change their minds about the Iraqi threat. The invasion of Iraq was sold to the American people not by making them think together so much as by making both proponents and opponents of the war move their lips together: WMD, WMD, WMD. The collective chanting of this phrase in the mass media echoed and scaled up the participatory patriotic singing conducted in 1917–1918 by 'Four-Minute Men' in public squares across the country.

Readers familiar with contemporary International Relations scholarship may have noticed that my argument dovetails with two theoretical innovations that have gained resonance in the discipline in recent decades. First, my claim that the chanting of 'weapons of mass destruction' performed a speech act evokes the concept of securitisation (Wæver 1995) which theorises that national security threats do not exist prior to language; rather, an issue becomes a threat by being named as such. More specifically, an issue becomes successfully 'securitised' when state officials pronounce it a security threat and when an 'audience' accepts the officials' pronouncement. The case of Iraq's securitisation in 2003, that is, the successful elevation of the Iraqi issue to the level of a grave menace to US national security, suggests that proclaiming an object a security threat may take the form of 'repeated assertion of talking points'. Moreover, this case suggests that the audience's acceptance consists not only in being persuaded by securitising talk but also, importantly, in actively participating in the performance of the talking points. Second, my analysis of the selling of the Iraq War to the American public dovetails with the 'practice turn' in International Relations theory (Adler and Pouliot 2011). The underlying intuition of the practice turn is that 'social realities – and international politics – are constituted by human beings acting in and on the world' (Cournot, n.d.). Human beings, in other words, form their beliefs and knowledge about the world through routine performance of material practices. Informed by this perspective, critics of Wæver's theorisation argued that objects/issues become securitised not through speech so much as through routinised performance of material practices 'such as programming algorithms, routine collection of data, and looking at CCTV footage' (Huysmans 2011, 372). My analysis suggests that securitisation performed in speech and securitisation performed in material practice are not mutually exclusive. The social reality of Iraq as being an existential security threat was shaped at once by the repetitive uttering of the words and by the material acts of lips moving and fingers tapping on keyboards together: WMD, WMD, WMD.

I conclude this section by quoting from a magazine column published shortly after the invasion of Iraq. At the time, a noisy and acrimonious debate was taking place on whether Iraq truly possessed weapons of mass destruction and, if it didn't, whether the claims of the administration were a lie or merely the product of an unintentional intelligence failure. Amid the din of the debate, Michael Kinsley was the only voice who recognised WMD for the securitising speech act that it was (even if he did not use this term).

> By now, WMD have taken on a mythic role in which fact doesn't play much of a part. The phrase itself – 'weapons of mass destruction' – is more like an incantation than a description of anything in particular. The term is a new one to almost everybody, and the concern it officially embodies was on almost no one's radar screen until recently. Unofficially, 'weapons of mass destruction' are to George W. Bush what fairies were to Peter Pan. He wants us to say, 'We DO believe in weapons of mass destruction. We DO believe. We DO'. If we all believe hard enough, they will be there. And it's working (Kinsley 2003).

With Kinsley, I argue that the incessant incantation of 'weapons of mass destruction' by the Bush administration, and the ricocheting of the phrase through the echo chamber of the mass media, emptied it of any specific meaning. Just as the repetition of liturgical texts serves to divert the worshipper's mind from his worldly situation and to affirm the axioms of his belief, so did the incantation of 'WMD' make Americans take the existence of these weapons as an article of faith, distracting the American mind from the realities of the Middle East. Moreover, just as the chanting of a mantra lifts the chanter above material reality and promotes the actualisation of the idea being uttered, so did the collective chant 'weapons of mass destruction' rhetorically create the Iraqi threat as much as it referred to such a threat.

Conclusion

In this chapter, I called attention to a central element of post-truth culture: the displacement of reality-based arguments by reality-shaping repetition of talking points, taglines, and catchphrases. I argued that the birth of this culture may be traced back to the propaganda campaign launched by the Wilson administration in 1917 to rally the US public behind the US intervention in the Great War. Following the campaign's success, the propaganda methods it employed – including, prominently, the repetitive spouting of catchphrases – were perfected in commercial marketing and political campaigning only to be reapplied to the marketing of foreign wars. The Bush Administration's 2002–2003 campaign to sell the Iraq War to the US public through repeating the phrase 'weapons of mass destruction' echoed and outperformed the anti-German chants of the Wilson Administration's 'Four-Minute Men'. The choral chanting of WMD, WMD, WMD by the Bush administration, the media, and the public had little to do with communicating objective facts about an Iraqi threat. Instead, the chorus successfully securitised Iraq, singing the threat into existence.

Figure 4.1 – Frequency of 'Weapons of Mass Destruction' in the Wall Street Journal, 1980–2003

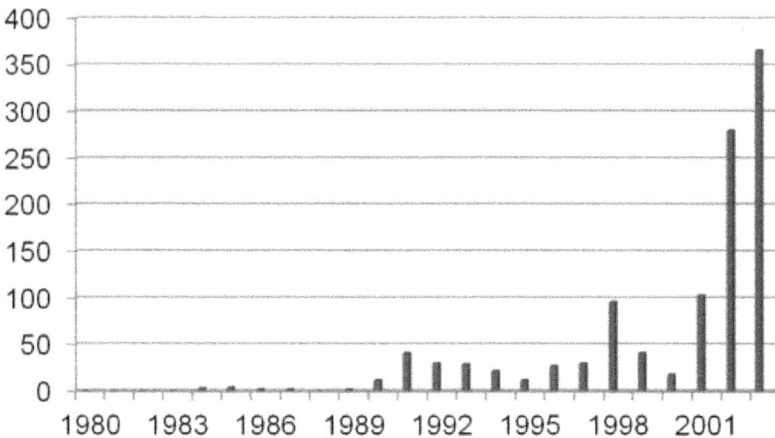

Figure 4.2 – Monthly frequencies of 'Weapons of Mass Destruction' in major US publications during the run up to the 2003 Iraq War

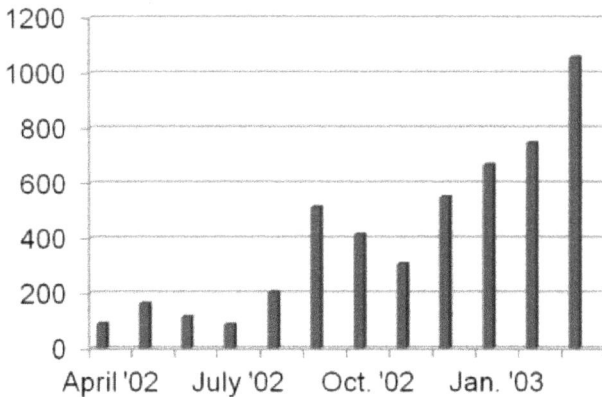

References

Adler, Emanuel, and Vincent Pouliot, eds. 2011. *International Practices*. New York: Cambridge University Press.

Austin, J. L., and James O. Urmson. 2009. *How to Do Things with Words*. 2nd ed., [Repr.]. Cambridge, Mass: Harvard Univ. Press.

Baudrillard, Jean. 1994. *Simulacra and Simulation*. Ann Arbor: University of Michigan Press.

Cook, Guy. 1992. *The Discourse of Advertising*. New York: Routledge.

Cournot, Jérémie. n.d. 'The Practice Turn in International Relations Theory'. In *Oxford Research Encyclopedia of International Studies*. https://oxfordre. com/internationalstudies/view/10.1093/acrefore/9780190846626.001.0001/ acrefore-9780190846626-e-113

Huysmans, Jef. 2011. 'What's in an Act? On Security Speech Acts and Little Security Nothings'. *Security Dialogue* 42 (4–5): 371–83.

Johnson, Catherine. 2012. *Branding Television*. New York: Routledge.

Kennedy, David M. 2004. *Over Here: The First World War and American Society*. 25th anniversary ed. New York: Oxford University Press.

Kinsley, Michael. 2003. 'Low Opinion: Did Iraq Have Weapons of Mass Destruction? It Doesn't Matter'. *Slate*, June 19, 2003. https://slate.com/news-and-politics/2003/06/did-iraq-have-weapons-of-mass-destruction-it-doesn-t-matter.html

Luntz, Frank I. 2007. *Words That Work: It's Not What You Say, It's What People Hear*. 1st ed. New York: Hyperion.

Marcuse, Herbert. 1991. *One-Dimensional Man: Studies in the Ideology of Advanced Industrial Society*. Boston: Beacon Press.

Oren, Ido, and Ty Solomon. 2013. 'WMD: The Career of a Concept'. *New Political Science* 35 (1): 109–35. https://doi.org/10.1080/07393148.2012.754683.

———. 2015. 'WMD, WMD, WMD: Securitisation through Ritualised Incantation of Ambiguous Phrases'. *Review of International Studies* 41 (2): 313–36. https://doi.org/10.1017/S0260210514000205.

Peterson, Peter G. 2009. *The Education of an American Dreamer: How a Son of Greek Immigrants Learned His Way from a Nebraska Diner to Washington, Wall Street, and Beyond*. 1st ed. New York: Twelve.

Popkin, Samuel L. 2012. *The Candidate: What It Takes to Win, and Hold, the White House*. New York: Oxford University Press.

Rifkin, Glenn. 1991. 'At 100, Public Relations' Pioneer Criticizes Some of His Heirs'. *New York Times*, December 30, 1991.

Suskind, Ron. 2004. 'Faith, Certainty and the Presidency of George W. Bush'. *New York Times Sunday Magazine*, October 17, 2004. https://www.nytimes.com/2004/10/17/magazine/faith-certainty-and-the-presidency-of-george-w-bush.html

Wæver, Ole. 1995. 'Securitization and Desecuritization'. In *On Security*, 46–86. New York: Columbia University Press.

5

Beyond Post-Truth: I-War and the Desire to be an Ethical All-American

HASMET M. ULUORTA

Academic literature, media coverage, and social media posts suggest that entire groups of individuals within the United States set truth aside and instead react incorrectly to fake news (see Bakir and McStay 2018; Polletta and Callahan 2019), or through conspiracy theories (see Hellinger 2019; Chebrolu 2021), or inauthentically because they are 'woke' (see Brian 2020; Kanai and Gill 2021) or have fallen prey to 'cultural Marxism' (see Jamin 2018; Mirrlees 2018). These conclusions are problematic and require a rethinking of the idea of the so-called post-truth age. At a minimum, the assertions themselves are post-truths predicated, as a matter of course, on a caricature of others and their worldview. More importantly, they fail to understand the elusiveness of truth and the complexity of knowing in a time when information flows have expanded, diversified, and quickened while other information flows are visibly constrained, noticeably blocked, and semi-hidden. But the focus on post-truth closes off deeper issues arising in American politics and society. Why should we assume the other needs to 'wake up' to the truth? Put another way, why do those that accuse the other person of being seduced by fake news, cultural Marxism and so forth assume that they have sole-possession of the truth? Why does the person who assumes a monopoly on the truth take up the position of moral superiority and of being more patriotic? Why do these same people assume that they are representative of the 'real America' while those others are actively working to destroy the nation? Why does the exposure to fact-checking, scientific testing and verification, and the consequent debunking of these post-truths, as lies, result not in their abandonment, but in many cases the dismissal and the reaffirmation of those debunked truths?

To answer these questions, I introduce seven Lacanian concepts used to understand the formation of the subject: the mirror-stage, the split subject, the big Other, the real/imaginary/symbolic, fantasy, topology, and specific traits. The seven provide a solid means of engaging with Lacanian theory by understanding key concepts to help anchor and situate oneself within this literature. For the purposes of this chapter, the seven concepts form a core to help facilitate a better understanding of the subject-in-formation from a Lacanian perspective. What is required, I argue, is an understanding of the subject that desires to believe in belief more now than before. In doing so, a much deeper and historically rooted problematic surfaces within the American polity that has destructive implications within the United States and is of global concern. Drawing on the distinction between knowledge and truth, I argue that American culture is calling forth an ontological form of warfare. This type of warfare is expressed through a warrior identification described as 'I-War'. I-War signifies a specific distorted form of American subjectivity. It contorts an already existing impossibility; namely being an ethical citizen of the United States or more colloquially being an ethical All-American. To resolve this impossibility of being an ethical All-American, the I-War identification necessitates a topological worldview where the gap between knowledge and truths is held together through fantasy, specific traits, and enjoyed aggressivity which only then manifests as adherence to and propagation of post-truths.

The first part of this chapter discusses the theory of the subject from a Lacanian perspective. It establishes the subject as a split subject whose desire for completion renders it split between nothingness and something offered through the social authority referred to as the big Other. The second section applies this theoretical understanding to the contemporary United States by discussing the ethical All-American identification which is comprised of three dominant social authorities or big Others: the capitalist, the religious-moral, as well as the nationalist-patriotic. The third section discusses the shift away from the ethical All-American to an I-War identification that has come to dominate American subject formation within the contemporary American neoliberal symbolic order-disorder (Lushetich 2019). While this is most closely associated with the Presidency of Donald Trump who, in retrospect, was the first I-War president, it only represents a particular culmination and not an ebbing of I-War. I conclude by suggesting that the claim that post-truths are solely attributable to Trump supporters/conservative Americans is not accurate. Nor will it serve to be productive in addressing any of the intensifying crises within the United States. Rather the focus on post-truths and the discarding of entire groups of individuals as deplorables can only result in irreparable harm, nationally and globally.

Subject identification: I am (not) (t)here

I begin with a brief exercise. Find a full-length mirror and stand before it. What do you see? Are you there in the mirror or are you standing before the mirror? You might say that you are both. If you are both, does this mean that what you see in the mirror is a subject like the person standing before the mirror? Maybe the image in the mirror is an object like other objects you look at, and see? How is it possible to describe the image of you in the mirror? Does your necessity to use language encapsulate what you see? Might there, for example, be a word that exists in your second language that better explains that something you see? This is the puzzle of subjectivity that Lacanians present, and it is the entry point into this chapter and to an expanded understanding of post-truths focusing on becoming a subject.

Lacan rejects any notion of the singular liberal autonomous subject. In its place is what Lacan refers to as the barred subject denoted by the symbol S with a line through it — $. To understand the split subject Lacan introduces and re-works Freud's mirror stage. At its most elementary level the mirror stage reveals a spatial gap between the viewer and what they view in the mirror. What is reflected in the mirror is the ego forming a false self because you can never be a cohesive self when your only way to experience selfhood is through this unbridgeable division. In other words, in seeing yourself, you identify with what is not you resulting in two distinct mis-recognitions or mis-knowings of the self.

Internally, as Bruce Fink (1995, 45) notes, '[t]he splitting of the I into ego (false-self) and unconscious brings into being a surface, in a sense, with two sides: one that is exposed and one that is hidden'. The ego in this instance is the effect of images. It has an imaginary function whereby the image that we see is that of wholeness, mastery and cohesiveness. The ego promotes and maintains this illusion of wholeness, coherence, and mastery (Homer 2005). The mirror experiment is useful in helping to visualise and make sense of this split subject, but it remains a crude analogy. A more accurate portrayal is that of a Möbius strip as it shifts away from a binary structure. What is revealed is a single form where tracing from one side of the strip brings about the other side without breaking the line. This topographical perspective of the subject provides an understanding of the gap within individuals and how the conscious and unconscious remain united and manifest as subject. In this narcissistic moment fantasies of control and permanence of self become the bedrock by which the individual understands their place in the world. I develop this further later in the chapter.

The mirror stage then provides a clear visualisation that I, as subject, am external to me. While one's ego maintains the lie of singularity and cohesion it can only do so by viewing the self in the mirror as an object. It is me but not me, as the image in the mirror is separated from the viewing self. What one views is outside of oneself and cannot then be the subject. It can only be described as an object that I do not have agency over. Lacan (2006, 78) describes it is an 'armor of an alienating identity that will mark [sic] his entire mental development with its rigid structure'. This misknowing renders the subject as a rival to itself. What is seen is an ideal-ego or idealised-I. The idealised-I that is on display within the mirror is that which, I desire, everyone to recognise as me. Put differently, this is what I desire to be and how I desire to be gazed upon and recognised as a subject by the big Other (and the others). This becomes a more profound paradox, as this requires one to be the object of the big Other's desire without fully knowing what the big Other desires of me.

The gap between the I that sees, and the object reflected in the mirror, is characterised by an irreducible lack. It is a lack of subjectivity. It is a lack of completion as there is no final point. And it is a lack of control, as the power of recognition rests with the big Other. Complicating this further for the subject is not knowing what exactly the big Other desires of me and what I must be within the big Other's gaze in order to exist (Roberts 2005). The big Other does not refer to the postcolonial other. Instead, it forms the discourse and law that structures individual desire (Homer 2005). To restate the argument thus far, subjectivity arises from outside and from something other than the subject and we now can add it does not arise directly from the big Other nor is it transcendental.

To make sense of this Lacanian psychoanalysis introduces three overlapping registers: the real, the imaginary and the symbolic. The real is that which cannot be represented since representation implies an immediate transference to the other registers. Aspects of the real, of the external flow, are necessarily internalised and bracketed to be understood. In doing so aspects of the real are necessarily transposed into the symbolic and imaginary registers. In other words, the world is only available to us in purposeful reflection. What, for example, happened on 11 September 2001? This irruption of the real is only available to us through the overlapping imaginary and symbolic registers. For many it was the President's explanations on that day and subsequently with the address to a joint session of Congress on 20 September 2011 that transformed the real into the imaginary and symbolic registers. President Bush used words such as evil, acts of terror, and mass murder to identify the perpetrators and situate their criminal acts. The President explained why the shocking acts were carried out, indicating that they occurred because the United States was, 'the brightest beacon for freedom in the world' (PBS News Hour 2021a) and that '[t]hey hate our freedom: our freedom of religion, our freedom of speech, our freedom to vote and assemble and disagree with each other' (PBS News Hour 2021b).

The imaginary, then, is the realm of identification and idealisation and is made visible within the optical model of the mirror stage. The mirror exercise above denotes both the importance and the overlap of the symbolic order as it structures the imaginary. The symbolic, is associated with symbols such as language, images and codes. More importantly, the symbolic is the authority and the law of the big Other. It follows that the symbolic is of utmost importance as language is the only way the subject can be a subject, but that language pre-dates the subject and is bound up in the dominant understandings within societies. The subject is a divided subject caught between the imaginary/symbolic and their desire for subjective wholeness. The wholeness is that extra bit that escapes capture or what Lacanians refer to as object *a*.

As discussed above, the subject lacks any means of knowing the desire of the big Other, which itself is incomplete and changes. Subject formation, therefore, is dominated by lack in both the subject and the mirrors. The mirrors are characterised by lack, as they cannot suppress the irruptions of the real nor can they adequately represent the real (Stravrakakis 1999, 51–54.) Anxiety then is associated with the desire of the big Other and it escalates when one has the feeling that they have the possibility of becoming the ultimate object of (the big Other's) desire.

In this chapter, I focus my analysis on the overlapping of the imaginary and the symbolic as the mirror phase, that moment when the individual recognises themselves as exterior to themselves (e.g., as reflected in image and the law of the big Other). In that instant of self-misrecognition, that is, of epistemological construction in the mirror the 'I' becomes a non-subject, an entity divided between a physical body and the idealised image (or idealised-I) contained within the mirror's image of the self and the discourse of the big Other (see also Kirsten Campbell 2004 and Kaja Silverman 1992).

The ethical all-American: Truth not knowledge

Neoliberalism institutionalised with the election of Ronald Reagan in 1980, is constituted by three mirrors that hail and signify 'reality' for the non-subject. Reflecting the law of the big Other, these mirrors are the capitalist-market, nationalist-patriotic and religious-moral mirrors. This forms the idealised-I that I refer to as the ethical All-American (Uluorta 2016). The three mirrors provide an objective ordering and a degree of ontological certainty predicated on the perception that the mirrors pertain to natural laws forming a transcendental truth outside of politics (and human intervention). The capitalist-market mirror conforms to the natural law of the market governed through the invisible hand that necessitates the truism of competitiveness. The religious-moral mirror is rooted in the law of God requiring adherents to the truism of the freedom of choice. While the nationalist-patriotic mirror is understood to be connected to the truth of American pre-eminence and exceptionalism. The desire, on the part of the hailed non-subject, to be an ethical All-American is a moral authority that can also be understood in its negative form. By refusing the lure of the big Others within the mirrors, one finds oneself cast as un-American. Failing to respond to the truth of the capitalist-market mirror marks one as a communist/socialist. To reject, or to make an unethical choice, imparts one as immoral within the religious-moral mirror. Failure to heed the truth of American exceptionalism, within the nationalist-patriotic mirror, marks one as a traitor.

The shift, presented here, from a singular mirror that is typical in Lacanian scholarship, to three mirrors is worth noting. Doing so provides an answer to the question about the ability of American neoliberalism to withstand significant shocks while retaining widespread legitimacy over the past 40-plus years. The rallying cry of the majority has not been to end neoliberalism, but to call for more neoliberalism (e.g., Tea Party Movement) or with a caveat of minor modifications (e.g., Atari democrats, Trump supporters). Adding to the above discussion on the Lacanian approach, the three mirrors intensify the desire to be an ethical All-American through qualities of repetition, distortion, and deflection.

Repetition is straightforward, as new technologies such as 24-hour news networks, social media, talk-radio, podcasts provide the means to reaffirm and maintain the big Other as consistent or in Lacanian terms without lack. Distortion highlights the desire we have for others to see us as ethical All-Americans. In this way, the big Other represented in the three mirrors becomes part of me. One can prove to others that they are the ethical All-American by being seen to be watching the right news, by following and sharing the right personalities on social media and informing our circle of friends and family that we listen to the right podcasts. In so doing, we participate in distorting our and other's reality for purposes that relate to our desire for subjective completion rather than simply noting the truth or expressing one's knowledge.

Deflection relates to how the mirrors do not provide a straightforward way to understand an issue and one's positioning. In other words, an economic issue does not have to operate through the capitalist-market mirror but could just as easily hail the non-subject through the religious-moral and/or nationalist-patriotic mirrors. The term globalising economy during the Clinton presidency provides a useful example. The shocks of (manufacturing) job losses were explained away through the capitalist-market mirror as the reality of living in a global economy. The nationalist-patriotic mirror though, repositioned this to be a struggle with Team USA competing against Team France and American exceptionalism preordaining American victory. The religious-moral mirror invoked the idea of the entrepreneur, as hero, requiring freedom to compete using the invisible hand as their only guide. This becomes especially clear, for example, as the Tea Party Movement would espouse this religious-moral truism to challenge the legitimacy of the Bush administration's passage of the Emergency Economic Stabilization Act of 2008 (Meckler and Martin 2012).

Repetition, distortion, and deflection partially obscure the fact that the big Others are incomplete. The non-subject avoids the trauma of this lack through fantasy. As Jodi Dean (2005, 13) posits,

> fantasy binds me to a certain set of relations. It structures and confines my thinking and acting such that my desires attach me to seemingly inescapable hierarchical relations or patterns of domination. The possibility of enjoyment that the fantasy holds open makes it very difficult for me to resist or break out of the situation in which I find myself.

The mirror stage reveals that one cannot be oneself. Instead, one is condemned to be a split-subject that requires the maintenance of a fantasy of subjective completion through adherence to the three mirrors that are also incomplete. In this way, fantasy does double duty as the inability of the symbolic to symbolise the real is masked through fantasy.

Lacan identifies two basic fantasies of the non-subject. The first is that someone or something wants to steal the enjoyment I will receive by being an ethical All-American. The often-repeated truism, the terrorists want to destroy our way of life is an example of this first type of fantasy. In this fantasy glossed over are the rising levels of social exclusion, income and wealth inequality within the United States as well as the consequences of poorly considered, designed and executed American foreign policy. A second fantasy assumes that the other is enjoying some form of excessive enjoyment which threatens the very possibility of me becoming an ethical All-American. President Reagan's reference to the supposed truth of 'welfare queens' sitting idly at home, engaging endlessly in extra-marital sex to collect higher child welfare benefits negated the real issues of deindustrialisation, racial segregation, and concentration of poor people geographically in hollowed out cities (Kandaswamy 2012). It is with this understanding of fantasy as a constitutive element of identity construction that political issues such as outsourcing, the rise of China and other competitors and so forth have been framed.

As Žižek (1989, 21) writes, the ideological is precisely, 'a social reality whose very existence implies the non-knowledge of its participants as to its essence'. What Žižek is noting is a distinction between knowledge and truth. Knowledge and truth are not indivisible. As it is often the case, we possess one and not the other. Truth and knowledge may more aptly be understood to be topologically related to one another, as there is a rubber logic that holds them together-apart. Often called qualitative mathematics, topology focuses on how different shapes can be stretched, twisted, bent, distorted and so forth in space without altering their intrinsic nature. Think, for example, of accusing someone of stretching the truth. What is being suggested with this phrase is that the truth remains foregrounded while the knowledge that supports the truth has receded. This allows the person to expand the truth of their statement as non-knowledge remains as an essence of the (stretched) truth.

Building on this notion of the rubber band, if one takes the band and pinches, twists, and pulls it what remains is still a rubber band. Another name for this twisted rubber band is a Möbius strip. This, for Lacanians, is the preferred way to understand the mirror phase. The visualisation metaphor of mirrors is useful as it allows one to see how the non-subject becomes themselves thanks to their linkage with the big Others of the capitalist-market, religious-moral and nationalist-patriotic. It has a critical limitation with deep implications. Understanding identification and subject formation through the concept of mirrors is also productive of the binary I/not I. Afterall, one might conclude that I look out to the mirrors and am reflected in them. It suggests then that I am an undivided self and could remedy any malady by rejecting the external impositions seen in the mirrors. The mirrors, however, are not opposite from us. Nor are they separated from us. We are divided from the start. This cannot be undone as this divide is part of the human condition. A topological understanding provides a more accurate understanding of this condition that the mirror metaphor simply cannot. In short, there is no 'I' that sees a reflection of the ethical-All American as out there. Instead, the non-subject is linked through the topological figure of the Möbius strip, where the outside connects with a singular line to its interior.

This is an important enhancement of the discussion thus far, as truth may be considered to be within the non-subject while knowledge is derived through tracing the line to the outside imaginary/symbolic or big Others. Recall that incursions of the real require discursive interpretation that arises within the imaginary/symbolic registers. The desire to be the ethical All-American demonstrates that the relationship between knowledge, truth and post-truth is not simple nor straightforward. Truth may precede knowledge, as we accumulate knowledge to arrive at the truths, we supposed existed. In other words, it is through the acquisition of knowledge that we arrive at truths. One can imagine a scenario where a truth is thought to be true (e.g., the earth is round), but what is required is the knowledge to prove the truth (e.g., observations of shadows by Eratosthenes around 250 BCE). In making known the knowledge of this truth the rubber logic reveals that the distance between truth and knowledge is compressed in this instance.

For our purposes, it is important to note that the opposite is also possible. Namely, one can possess truth without knowledge or what Žižek refers to as non-knowledge. This gap between truth and knowledge presents three impasses. First, as already alluded to, there is a necessary reliance on the big Others to eliminate the gap between truth and knowledge. In an age of instantaneous media, the power of the big Other is augmented through repetition, distortion, and deflection. The distance between the non-subject and the big Others is shortened to an almost constant hailing. Yet, this is not simply about truth (as opposed to falsehoods or lies), as it is about eliminating the incompleteness of the big Others and the resultant painful sense of lack within the non-subject. Seeking to bring knowledge and truth together may be more a desire to eliminate lack than it is to pursue truth or knowledge. Second, elimination of the lack may not require knowledge, but rather depend on fantasy. Our behaviours, motivated by our desire to be the ethical All-American, may be sustained as much by unconscious fantasy and racial fantasies as they might by conscious knowledge as discussed below. Third, the big Others that are supposed to know may be revealed as failing to maintain and adhere to truths required by the non-subject in order to fulfil their desire for wholeness.

I-War and symbolic demise

The everyday visibility of the stretch between knowledge and truth has triggered a shift in the desire to be an ethical All-American. This shift is I-War. I-War has come about due to the distanciated desire of the non-subject to, not only, be the ethical All-American but to also cloak the visible 'demise of the symbolic authority' of the capitalist-market, nationalist-patriotic and religious-moral mirrors (Žižek 1999, 322). The consequence of this demise has not resulted in a re-imagining of what it means to be an American in a globalising world with several socio-economic, geopolitical, and biospheric emergencies. Instead, the promotion and militant adherence to specific traits, re-doubling of fantasy, along with interpassive believing informs the desire to become an ethical All-American. Think here how the knowledge of American accomplishments are now stretched away from truths such as, we're number one and land of the free. They have become examples of specific traits that rely upon means, beyond knowledge, for their sustenance. The distance between truth and knowledge is such that I-War forms the basis for attaining and retaining the ethical All-American non-subject position. My argument should not be confused with a sort of evolution from one to another, or the supplanting of one and the rejection of another. Instead, the rubber logic, the möbius strip, suggests a distortion of the ethical All-American.

The emergence of the I-War non-subject corresponds most closely with the George W. Bush presidency. Key events include the 2003 invasion of Iraq, the 2006 Dubai Ports Deal, and the passage of the 2008 Emergency Economic Stabilization Act. All three of these have contributed to the demise of the symbolic order. Not only did activists engage in the largest anti-war protests, but the logic for the invasion continually shifted to the point where no logic prevailed or was accepted. Žižek (2004), drawing on Freud, refers to this shifting as the borrowed kettle where the multiplication of lies undermines certainty. I would add though that there was an important exception, namely those who believed the United States must act outside the law in order to produce the law. The Dubai Ports deal seen as a purely capitalist narrative of economic globalisation would be met with disgust as it was seen as running counter to both security and American exceptionalism. What was unconvincing was the Bush administration's insistence on national security through the waging of the War on Terror and the selling of what were perceived to be American-only and American strategic interests to a foreign firm. There can be no doubt as well that as the deal involved a company from the United Arab Emirates that this served to intensify objections. The events of the 2008 capitalist crisis, leading to the largest bailout in history by American taxpayers, would ultimately lead to both the Tea Party and Occupy Wall Street movements who openly challenged the symbolic order as being insufficient.

This growing tension between the hailing of the ethical All-American and the furthering gap that is productive of I-War may be expressed, for example, with a seemingly benign exchange between the 2008 Republican Presidential candidate John McCain and a would-be voter who stated, 'I don't trust Obama...He's an Arab'. McCain responded saying, 'No, ma'am, he's a decent, family man, a citizen that I just happen to have disagreements with' (Stewart 2018). This exchange reveals mis-knowing, as both are shocked by the other's response. McCain failed to understand the woman's sacrifice as she was seemingly overwrought by the inability of the symbolic order, represented here by McCain, to re-present as whole. As Derek Hook (2021) notes, the racist fantasy played out by the would-be voter was not simply of fear that Obama formed an illicit obstacle to being an ethical All-American. It was also a contradictory sense of enjoyment of hatred by the would-be voter as it was functioned to produce the ethical All-American social bond (Chebrolu 2020). McCain's response instead reminded the would-be voters of the lack within the symbolic that reaffirmed their own subjective lack further distancing them from attaining the ethical All-American identification and consequently marching them towards identification as I-War.

Taking this one step further, the movement towards I-War may be understood through the lens of nostalgia and difference. What McCain misrecognised was what President George W. Bush signified during this first term which was nostalgia. President Bush with his gaffes and seemingly folksy tone and presentation along with his stern responses to 9/11 harkened back to a simpler utopian past where the symbolic order was without lack, thereby making it seem possible to attain subjective completion as the ethical All-American. McCain in that exchange, and the eventual winner of the presidential election Barack Obama, signified openness to the unknown with the calamity of lack manifesting and thereby removing the possibility of subjective completion, cementing the drive to I-War. To further complicate this, it is clear that this reading is not complete without its reversal namely that former President Obama represented the possibility of attaining the ethical All-American and Bush the movement away. This is certainly possible. Nevertheless, the point is that the manifestation of intensifying insecurities quickly dissipated the possibilities of hope and change associated with President Obama. Lack and the symbolic demise would only intensify.

I-War: Belief and specific traits

Returning to the discussion of the rubber logic associated with truth and knowledge, we can identify the substance holding the two together-apart. Lacan suggests that a transcendental identification, such as the ethical All-American, is made possible with the articulation of specific traits (Haute 2002). These signifiers are fixed points allowing the non-subject the possibility of becoming the ethical All-American. At that very moment that the split subject identifies with the specific trait or signifier, the specific trait determines the subject entirely. In other words, the non-subject disappears under the signifier. Signifiers such as (but not limited to) beacon for democracy, a city upon a hill, competition, freedom, leader of the free world, and liberty are indicative of truths without the requirement of knowledge. The work done by specific traits, which conforms to the foregrounding of the I-War identification, is not simply the denial of the possibility of lack within the capitalist-market, religious-moral and nationalist-patriotic mirrors. Instead, it also compels the activation of the non-subject to assume that they are the originators of the laws once enunciated within the symbolic order. Politically the inability to become the ethical All-American requires the elimination of the other. I-war disavows the other's statements, claims and presence. Yet, in this attempt, what is disavowed is the non-subject's identification of an object of derision. The other is a made into a cartoon requiring that they be smacked, walloped, or woken up in order to be a real American.

President Trump has fundamentally altered the presidency as he is the first president of the I-War identification. Candidate Donald Trump brought attention to the widening demise in the symbolic order that blocked any possibility of being an ethical All-American. Trump (2016) announced, '[o]ur convention occurs at a moment of crisis for our nation. The attacks on our police, and the terrorism in our cities, threaten our very way of life. Americans watching this address tonight have seen the recent images of violence in our streets and the chaos in our communities'. He continued to speak about the economic decay across the United States, focusing on job losses and deindustrialisation. Identifying immigrants, corrupt politicians, globalists, and smart adversaries as the cause of the blockage, he called on their removal to Make America Great Again. He went on to say, 'I have a message for all of you. The crime and violence that today afflicts our nation will soon – and I mean very soon – come to an end. Beginning on January 20th, 2017, safety will be restored'. President Trump would be a lightning rod for those who insisted that the other stole their enjoyment of attaining the ethical All-American identification. Over this period, what would be on full display was the enjoyment supporters exuded in stating that their enjoyment had been stolen. More importantly for the manifestation of the I-War identification, came the unwavering faith in the truth of the specific traits as this made all of this possible.

While President Trump was electorally defeated in 2020, the I-War identification suggests a war with no beginning or end. I-War brings individuals as battlefield, the individual as the detonation. What is sought by the I-War identification is full-spectrum security – social, cultural, economic, geopolitical, spiritual, biological, and so forth. It is not an idyllic or utopian vision of a society without crime for example. It is a society seeking to regain that which was always impossible.

Conclusion

Post-truth came to dominate global headlines with the 2015 American presidential campaign, the subsequent presidency of Donald Trump along with the 2016 Brexit campaign in the United Kingdom. The term was selected in 2016 as the Oxford Dictionary's 'Word of the Year' and defined as, 'relating to or denoting circumstances in which objective facts are less influential in shaping public opinion than appeals to emotion and personal belief' (Oxford

Dictionaries 2016). I have argued that the Lacanian theorisation of subject formation as a split-subject challenges the assumed straight forward relationship between individuals and truth. Instead, as argued, individuals are split between three hailing mirrors informing them on how to be a subject. I have described that subject as the ethical All-American. Locating that identification within the American neoliberal symbolic order-disorder, I have suggested that the demise of the symbolic order to affirm this identification has resulted in the formation of a militant identity known as I-war. Those hailed as I-War assume themselves to be the originators of the symbolic law, of truths. Described as specific traits of the ethical All-American, these truths are thought to be transcendental in form and consequently exist outside the processes of knowledge formation. Consequently, knowledge is discounted and viewed as unimportant in the quest to affirm truths that underpin the possibility of subjecthood.

The significance of this analysis is that it lays visible that interventions, such as the New York Times in-depth explanation of how to evaluate fake news (Schulten and Brown 2017) or fact-checking (e.g., Politifact) that reveal claims to be false and banning content and users on social media platforms while important are inadequate to remedy the situation. It is not, however, a rejection of facts and expertise (see Nichols 2017). But rather more complex. Experts line up on all sides. How to decide? How to know which expert or pundit or neighbour presents the truth? This cannot be glossed over by patronising and caricaturing others as believers in post-truth, fake news and so forth. Therein lies the deeper danger to dismiss, to try and show one's position as superior because the other is whatever negative descriptor one can muster. These are all fantasies based on the assumption of becoming the ethical All-American without another. The truth, for the subject, will always remain divided and necessarily incomplete because the subject itself is barred from knowing the complete truth of their own subjectivity. It is only by understanding this that we can begin to build a different democracy that befits an era of massive information flows characterised by intensifying socio-economic, geopolitical, and biospheric emergencies.

The author would like to thank Dylan Cameron for his research assistance, on post-truths, populism, and American politics during the summer of 2021.

References

Andrejevic, Mark. 2013. *Infoglut*. New York, NY: Routledge.

Bailey, Lionel. 2009. *Lacan: A Beginner's Guide*. Oxford: Oneworld Publications.

Brian, Paul. 2020. 'Woke Crony Capitalism: Money meets left-wing ideology'. *The American Conservative*. Vol.19(6): 6–7.

Campbell, Kirsten. 2004. *Jacques Lacan and Feminist Epistemology*. New York: Routledge.

Chebrolu, E. 2021. 'The function and field of speech and language in white nationalist manifestoes'. *Lacan and Race: Racism, Identity, and Psychoanalytic Theory*, edited by Sheldon George and Derek Hook, 65–82. New York: Routledge.

Chebrolu, E. 2020. "Free speech and loss in white nationalist rhetoric." *First Amendment Studies*. Vol.54(2): 197–208.

Dean, Jodi. 2010. *Blog theory*. London, UK: Polity Press.

Fink, Bruce. 1995. *The Lacanian Subject: Between Language and Jouissance*. Princeton: Princeton University Press.

Haute, Philippe van. 2002. *Against Adaptation: Lacan's 'Subversion' of the Subject*, trans. Paul Crowe and Miranda Vankerk. New York: Other Press.

Hellinger, Daniel C. 2019. *Conspiracies and Conspiracy Theories in the Age of Trump*. New York: Palgrave Macmillan.

Hook, Derek. 2021. 'Pilfered pleasure: on racism as "the theft of enjoyment"'. *Lacan and Race: Racism, Identity, and Psychoanalytic Theory*, edited by Sheldon George and Derek Hook, 35-50. New York: Routledge.

Homer, Sean. 2005. *Jacques Lacan*. London: Routledge.

Iversen, Margaret. 2007. *Beyond Pleasure: Freud, Lacan, Barthes*. University Park: Pennsylvania State University Press.

Jamin, Jérôme. 2018. 'Cultural Marxism: A Survey'. *Religion Compass*. Vol.12(1-2): 1–17.

Kandaswamy, Priya. 2012. 'Gendering Racial Formation'. In *Racial Formation in the Twenty-First Century*, edited by Daniel Martinez HoSang, Oneka LaBennett and Laura Pulido, 23–43. Berkeley: University of California Press.

Kanai, Akane and Rosalind Gill. 2021. "Work? Affect, Neoliberalism, Marginalized Identities and Consumer Culture." *New Formations*. Vol. 102: 10–27.

Lacan, Jacques. 1953. 'Some Reflections on the Ego'. *International Journal of Psycho-Analysis*. No.34: 13–15.

Lacan, Jacques. 2006. 'The Mirror Stage as Formative of the *I* Function as Revealed in Psychoanalytic Experience'. In Écrits*: the first complete edition in English*. Translated by Bruce Fink, 75–81. New York: W.W. Norton & Company.

Lushetich, Natasha. 2019. 'The Performative Constitution of Liberal Totalitarianism on Facebook'. In Žižek *and Performance*, edited by Broderick Chow and Alex Mangold, 94–109. New York: Palgrave Macmillan.

McGowan, Todd. 2004. *The end of dissatisfaction? Jacques Lacan and the emerging society of enjoyment*. Albany: State University of New York Press.

McGowan, Todd (with Paul Eisenstein). 2012. *Rupture: On the Emergence of the Political*. Evanston: Northwestern University Press.

Meckler, Mark and Jenny Beth Martin. 2012. *Tea Party Patriots: The second American Revolution*. New York, NY: Henry Holt.

Mirrlees, Tanner. 2018. The Alt-Right's Discourse of "Cultural Marxism": A Political Instrument of Intersectional Hate'. *Atlantis Journal*. 39.1: 49–69.

Nichols, Tom. 2017. *The Death of Expertise: The Campaign Against Established Knowledge and Why it Matters*. New York: Oxford University Press.

Oxford Dictionaries. 2016. 'Word of the Year 2016 is....' https://languages.oup.com/word-of-the-year/2016/

PBS News Hour. (2021a). 'President George. W. Bush's address to the nation after September 11, 2001 attacks'. *YouTube*, 4:24. August 19, 2021. https://www.youtube.com/watch?v=WA8-KEnfWbQ

PBS News Hour. (2021b). 'President George. W. Bush's address to a joint session of Congress following 9/11 – Sept. 20, 2001'. *YouTube*, 35:13. Sept 03, 2021. https://www.youtube.com/watch?v=ZF7cPvaKFXM

Polletta, Francesca and Jessica Callahan. 2019. 'Deep Stories, Nostalgia Narratives, and Fake News: Storytelling in the Trump Era'. In *Politics of Meaning/Meaning of Politics: Cultural Sociology of the 2016 U.S. Presidential Election*, edited by Jason L. Mast and Jeffrey C. Alexander, 55–73. New York: Palgrave Macmillan.

Pound, Marcus. 2008. Žižek: *A (Very) Critical Introduction*. Cambridge: William B. Eerdmans Publishing Company.

Roberts, John. 2005. 'The Power of the 'Imaginary' in Disciplinary Processes'. *Organization*. 12(5): 619–642.

Schulten, Katherine and Christy Brown. 2017. 'Evaluating Sources in a "Post-Truth" World: Ideas for Teaching and Learning About Fake News'. *New York Times*, January 19, 2017. https://www.nytimes.com/2017/01/19/learning/lesson-plans/evaluating-sources-in-a-post-truth-world-ideas-for-teaching-and-learning-about-fake-news.html

Silverman, Kaja 1992. *Male Subjectivity at the Margins*. London and New York: Routledge.

Stavrakakis, Yannis. 1999. *Lacan and the political*. London: Routledge.

Stewart, Emily. 2018. 'Watch John McCain defend Barack Obama against a racist voter in 2008'. *Vox*, September 1, 2018. https://www.vox.com/policy-and-politics/2018/8/25/17782572/john-mccain-barack-obama-statement-2008-video

Uluorta, Hasmet M. 2016. 'The Tea Party: An Ethical All-American Performance'. In *Dissent! Refracted: Histories, Aesthetics and Cultures of Dissent,* edited by Ben Dorfman, 95–116. New York: Peter Lang.

Van Schoor, Eric P. 2000. 'A Sociohistorical View of Group Psychotherapy in the United States: The Ideology of Individualism and Self-Liberation'. *International Journal of Group Psychotherapy*. 50(4): 437–454.

Žižek, Slavoj. 1989. *The sublime object of ideology*. New York: Verso Books.

Žižek, Slavoj. 1998. 'Cyberspace, or How to Traverse the Fantasy in the Age of the Retreat of the Big Other'. *Public Culture* 10(3): 483–513.

Žižek, Slavoj. 1999. *The ticklish subject*. London, UK: Verso.

Žižek, Slavoj. 2004. *Iraq: The borrowed kettle*. London, UK: Verso.

Žižek, Slavoj. 2007. *How to read Lacan*. New York: W.W. Norton.

6

European Crises and Right-Wing Populism: The Case of Lega Nord

IRENE VIPARELLI AND EVANTHIA BALLA

The link between post-truth and right-wing populism has been investigated under various lenses, such as through populist discourses, social media and global politics. In the European Union, populism, despite not being a new phenomenon, has gained an alarming share of the electorate during the continent's long period of crises and distress in recent years following the Eurozone crisis, the refugee crisis and the Brexit disintegration challenge. Under this prism, a series of questions arise: What is the relationship between the rise of right-wing populism and the European crises? How has the post-truth contributed to the increase of right-wing populism in Europe? This chapter first demonstrates the legitimacy gap, and the related distrust of the European project, which heightened during the aforementioned crises and offered a 'fruitful field' for right-wing populism to gain greater relevance and influence by openly using anti-EU rhetoric. Secondly, it argues that while in a 'regime of shared truth', right-wing populism never succeeded in gaining a broader consensus. Yet, in the post-truth age, it offered an array of unrestrained 'truths', extensively using social media as a key platform for direct communication with the public, threatening democracy itself.

This study adopts a threefold narrative. Firstly, it offers a conceptual analysis of right-wing populism in a post-truth age. This section focuses on the definitions and links between European right-wing populism and the post-truth. The second section discusses the relationship between the crises, the rise of populism and the post-truth age. It shows that since the beginning of the twenty-first century, the European Monetary Union's (EMU) weaknesses, as well as the financial and refugee crises were capitalised by right-wing populist parties. Populist right-wingers thus took advantage of this decline of trust to mobilise economic polarisation and nativist sentiments, spreading a particular anti-EU rhetoric. However, in a post-truth environment, right-wing populist parties have been able to spread their political rhetoric as never before, extensively using social media as a platform for direct, yet unrestrained, communication with the public. This has resulted in unprecedented electoral success at national and European levels – further challenging democratic values and the European project itself. The third part focuses on a case study of the Italian Lega Nord – which was not originally a right-wing populist party, instead belonging to a populist and ethno-regionalist party family rooted under a pro-EU and anti-statism ideology. However, in order to respond to the challenges of European integration, the party has progressively loosened its original features and joined the right-wing populist party family. Therefore, Lega Nord's transformation helps shed light on the link between the accretion of right-wing populism and the European crises. Lega Nord's Matteo Salvini has been the European leader that has used social media the most in his political campaigns over recent years, reaching more than 3,000,000 followers in 2018 (Cervi 2020). Such a successful strategy has allowed Lega to reach the best electoral results in its history in the national election of 2018 and in the European elections of 2019. In this vein, Lega shows how the post-truth age has allowed the spreading of right-wing populist ideology as never before, threatening European democratic values and the European Union political project.

Right-wing populism in a post-truth age: A conceptual analysis

Right-wing populism and post-truth are heterogeneous concepts that merge in contemporary global politics, challenging democratic political regimes and values. Thus, before focusing on the main issue of this chapter, it is useful to develop a conceptual analysis clarifying the link between the two phenomena.

Although a general definition of populism is still lacking in the academic literature, from a theoretical perspective, populism has been conceptualised by some key terms (Caiani and Graziano 2021, 2–3):

- as a 'political rhetoric' that is marked by public sentiments of disappointment;
- as an 'ideology', which considers society being segregated into two antagonistic groups: 'the people' vis-à-vis 'the elite',
- and as 'a type of organisation', a political strategy, dominated by the presence of a charismatic leadership.

With regards to right-wing populism, two further features have to be added: authoritarianism, related to law-and-order doctrines, and nativism, related to the importance of the homogeneity and the purity of the nation (Bergmann 2020; Heinisch, Massetti and Mazzoleni 2020) – implying an attitude of repulsion and exclusion of the 'aliens'. Finally, in the framework of the European Union, due to the link between the deepening integration process and the limitation of the state's sovereignty, right-wing populism has gained a further feature – Euroscepticism.

Quoting the Oxford definition of post-truth, McIntyre (2018) describes it as the framework in which public opinion is more shaped by emotional discourses than by truth. Indeed, the post-truth age occurs when – 'depending on what one wants to be true – some facts matter more than others' (McIntyre 2018). While strategic extraction of partial facts from its context enables the 'fabrication of a reality' in agreement with personal desires or beliefs, objective facts hampering personal realisation are dismissed. Social media has played a central role in the advent of post-truth. It has multiplied the sources of information while also allowing content to be more quickly disseminated. Moreover, virtual platforms follow the same logic of the post-truth age: algorithms select content and produce 'alternative information ecosystems' (Cosentino 2020) according to users' interests and feelings. Thus, social media becomes a type of 'market of truths' (Harsin 2018), where everyone may choose the most convenient one, without any kind of gatekeeper (Corvi 2020), i.e. without a process of content filtration and editorial control on the accountability of sources. Hence, social media contributes to blurring the boundaries between truths and lies, creating a dis-information system where it is almost impossible to discern between real facts and fake news. Therefore, as McIntyre points out, 'what seems new in the post-truth era is a challenge not just to the idea of knowing reality but to the existence of reality itself' (McIntyre 2018).

Nonetheless, Oxford dictionary's definition of 'post-truth' is not exhaustive, lacking the deep causes of the phenomenon – much of which has been explored in prior chapters. Social media may be used to share knowledge, scientific issues, news, information, and false and distorted representations of reality. Therefore, why does the post-truth occur? Why have communicational potentialities of social media become a driver for negationist movements or, as it is the case in this article, for right-wing populist discourses? According to Bennett and Livingston (2021), analyses only addressing new communicational technologies 'tend to focus on the symptoms and not on the causes'. The latter must be searched out in the deep crisis of what Foucault named a 'regime of truth'. As Cosentino (2018) and Harsin (2015) point out, what is really at stake in the rise of the 'post-truth regime' is not the opposition between a hypothetical objective reality and subjective emotions, but rather the loss of a shared 'truth', guaranteed by political institutions and by a narrow set of mainstream media. For Bennett and Livingston, the rise of the post-truth age results from a deep 'crisis of legitimacy of authoritative institutions' (Bennett and Livingston 2021, 4), which is rooted in the dominance of 'disinformation strategies' in political communication during the last decades. Political forces all over the world have systematically used communicational strategies which distort reality while searching for popular legitimacy to improve unpopular policies. This has resulted in a progressive loss of trust in democratic institutions, and in official information networks. Thus, social media has consolidated itself as an alternative information channel.

However, we argue that a communicational framework per se does not succeed in explaining the complexity of the post-truth age. As analysed later in the chapter, the European case sheds light on the essential link between the multiple crises that occurred during the beginning of the twenty-first century – the rise of populism and post-truth. Indeed, the European case in general, and the Italian case of Lega in particular, demonstrate that the political consequences of monetary union, as well as how the financial and refugee crises have progressively increased distrust in the EU project, determining a favourable framework for nationalist and nativist rhetoric of right-wing parties. The latter have constantly instrumentalised the structural contradictions of the European project and its critical conjunctures to improve their visibility as a way of gaining popular consensus. In the pre-post-truth age, the mainstream media were the main channel for political communication – and the democratic 'regime of truth' was still able to produce shared values. In such a context, the populist use of popular malaise had never succeeded in becoming a widespread and threatening phenomenon. Thus, right-wing populist parties were forced to maintain a 'defensive attitude' toward both the public sphere and democratic institutions (McDonnell and Werner 2019). During the last decade, the post-truth age has given the EU's right-wing populism a framework to grow. While the increase in popular disaffection in the European project enhances angry and feared citizen groups, social media allows right-wing populist parties to shift away from mediation of the public sphere and to establish a direct dialogue between political figures and their followers. Thus, through social news sources, right-wing populist forces have succeeded in 'mobilising angry publics around emotionally charged themes' (Bennett and Livingston 2021), such as regarding the financial or refugee crises. Therefore, they have constantly improved their visibility and increased their popular consensus, becoming a dangerous threat to Europe's multiculturalist and inclusive values.

According to Tumber and Waisbord (2021), there is a deep affinity between social media and right-wing populist rhetoric. However, the latter has succeeded in transforming the 'misinformation system', i.e. the domination of emotions and wills and the impossibility to discern truths from lies in social media, into a 'disinformation system' (Cosentino 2020). In this regard, they have built a political strategy based on the intentional manipulation of information for electoral goals. Thereby, right-wing populism has played a key role in the statement of post-truth as a fundamentally political problem, as a 'regime of post-truth' menacing western democracies.

European crises and the rise of populism

Although there has been a general appreciation for and adherence to the European integration project, legitimacy issues have become increasingly more noticeable as integration advanced. In turn, weak responses to crises further undermined public trust to the project itself. In these terms, the new century witnessed a new wave of populism and a reinforced anti-EU rhetoric (Mudde 2019). Thus, decisions made at the European level have become part of domestic political discourse which has incorporated a significant level of Euroscepticism (Newsome; Riddervold and Trondal 2021, 597; Lacey and Nicolaïdis 2020, 378). Thus, the EU's flaws and perceived weak responses to crises have echoed across the political spectrum of member states. In populist right-wing propaganda, Euroscepticism has been engineered around a division between European economic 'elites' and common 'people', having been fed by disinformation over the endangerment of migration to the supremacy of national identities. On the other hand, populism is not concerned with truth-telling. A simplistic claim of populism, 'you have your truth, I have mine', has also promoted polarisation (Waisbord 2018, 14). In addition, in the post-truth age, social media have been disseminating 'fact-less' information at a scale unparalleled in history. However, as Bennett and Livingston have claimed, 'putting the spotlight on social media alone misses deeper erosions of institutional authority' (2021, 5), and the broader picture of democratic disruption (Tumber and Waisbord 2021).

The creation of EMU in 1990 marked a significant point in terms of European integration. It indicated the transfer of sovereignty from a national to a supranational level in monetary policy, simultaneously creating new supranational institutions such as the European Central Bank and a common currency – a key symbol of a collective identity (Torres et al. 2004; Negri et al. 2020). The public initially perceived EMU as a technocratic project justified upon a macroeconomic rationale and led by bureaucrats and bankers. Likewise, member states' efforts to meet the eurozone's criteria implied that the national welfare state systems could be compromised to achieve budgetary discipline. This popular unease was well illustrated in the 2000 Danish and 2003 Swedish referenda that rejected the introduction of the euro as their official currency (Schmidtke 2004, 21; Dinan et al. 2017, 363). Schmidtke argues that in this background of uncertainty, the success of a variety of right-wing parties took place, based on a simplistic and populist form of protest (2004, 29). The right-wing populist rhetoric marked lines of division among a trustworthy nation state of 'people' and an untrustworthy

European undemocratically elected 'elite'. It also promoted anti-immigrant political propaganda, stoking fear over foreign and culturally different people, portraying them as potential terrorists or job takers, in other words as a threat to the purity and security of the nation state and its native population. However, as this was a period still dominated by mainstream media, with Euroscepticism being viewed as radical phenomenon rather than as a political reality, right-wing populism failed to gain a sufficient electorate.

The post-truth challenge becomes apparent following the 2008 Global Financial Crisis. As the authority and trustworthiness of European institutions deteriorated, citizens were left wandering and in quest for emotionally fulfilling alternatives – i.e. 'truths'. Indeed, the financial shock was dealt on a functional rather than a political rationale, with the ECB's procedures, bailouts and macro-economic supervision forming the main premises of the EU and Eurozone responses (Dinan et al. 2017, 6; Hooghe and Marks 2019, 1119). As a result, tough austerity measures in debt-burdened countries led to unprecedented levels of unemployment, as well as economic and social unrest, further shaking citizens' confidence to the problem-solving capacities of the EU. The moment was ideal for populists to once again promote division between the 'elite' (European technocrats) and 'the people'. Their rhetoric was oversimplistic and emotional and lacked depth and analysis over the 'causes and consequences' of the crisis itself, as questions over political weaknesses of the EMU per se had not been detailed. The emergence of social media in the same period allowed populists to rapidly communicate their rhetoric to and from the public, thus reaching wider audiences across borders. As Lehne points out, 'the speed, superficiality and interactive nature of social media make them very well suited to spread populist ideas' (2017).

While the financial crisis was still unfolding, Europe was about to encounter a new challenge. The Arab Spring and the political and social turmoil and civil wars it unleashed across North Africa and the Middle East resulted in unpreceded flows of refugees and migrants to Europe. In 2015 alone, 1.8 million irregular border-crossings into the EU were registered (Weber 2019, 135; Buonno 2017, 101–102). Security and economic concerns soon surrounded the issue while disagreements over the reception, the relocation and the limiting of refugees rose among member states (Weber 2019, 153–170). As a result, numerous states reinstalled border controls putting the free movement of people in the EU's Schengen area on hold – and in doing so challenging one of the Union's triumph projects. Moreover, key decisions, as with the EU-Turkey refugee deal, revealed a trend of intergovernmental bargaining with third countries as a response to crises, while neglecting any public consultation apparatus. Developments such as Frontex reinforcement through the creation of the European Coast and Board Guard and new hotspots could not undermine that trend (Schweiger 2017, 206; Webber 2019,

171). In many member states, the combination of the high importance of the migration issue together with widespread public dissatisfaction with the EU's management fuelled 'defensive nationalism' sentiments and cultural division. Thus, a fertile ground for the emergence of anti-EU, anti-refugee, and white supremacist parties was produced (Kriesi 2018, 38; Webber 2019, 172). As Hooghe and Marks put it 'the migration crisis touched a nerve of national identity' (2019, 1122). In 2016, the UK Independence Party (UKIP) and the elements of the Conservative Party in Britain advanced an anti-immigrant campaign that played a key role during Brexit. They endorsed the position that migrants were not only a threat to the nation's wellbeing and security, but also undermining to the national identity of local people (Outhwaite 2018; Mudde 2019, 125, 52; Coman et al. 2020, 22–23).

While during the 1900s and 2000s, right-wing populists had not achieved significant electoral results, having also failed to form a sole long-lasting European Parliament group, in the 2014 European elections they reached unprecedented power, with 73 out of the 751 elected Members of the European Parliament being radical right-wing populists (McDonnell and Werner 2019, 4). In 2015, they managed to form a coalition under the European of Nations and Freedom (ENF) group. Later, in the 2019 elections, the right-wing populist force appeared in even greater numbers, winning the majority of votes in Italy, France, Poland and Hungary (under the coalition of right-wing political party FIDESZ with the conservative Christian Democratic People's Party). On 8 April 2019, Salvini launched a far-right alliance aiming to form a powerful bloc at the European level, as will be discussed further in the next section. Under this prism, populism and Euroscepticism, in all their forms, no longer appeared as radical phenomena, but rather as a mainstreamed (Mudde 2019) political reality.

However, it was in the post-truth age that populist forces really managed to thrive and even form coalitions, further threatening democracy and the EU integration project itself. While in a regime of shared truth, political debates took place broadly within the framework of accepted values, norms and understandings – an array of emotional truths seem to predominate in the post-truth age. In the EU, the financial and the migrant crises accentuated public disappointment and reactions to the EU's structural flaws and further shook the trust on EU institutions. In this framework, populist right-wing parties managed to gain unconventional power, mobilising frustrated audiences around anti-EU, global elite conspiracies and nativism rhetoric. In this vein, social media provided an unlimited array of information that could be tailored according to people's beliefs and emotions (Bennett and Livingston 2021, Tumber and Waisbord 2021).

The Lega Nord case

Lega Nord was founded in 1991 by its charismatic leader Umberto Bossi, aiming at representing the interests of small and medium entrepreneurs of Northern Italy who felt undermined by the Italian political agenda. In this framework, the European Union represented its main ally against the Italian political elite. Thus, inspired by the neo-federalist theory of the Italian philosopher Gianfranco Miglio, Lega envisaged the foundation of an 'Europe of regions' based on economic liberalism and on the primacy of local autonomies over the State's sovereignty (Cento et al. 2001, 24–26; Tarchi 2015, 191–196). Moreover, the European identity complemented Lega's nativist discourse, symbolising the common values of the developed West against southern Italy's people, rhetorically identified with the Africans, that is, with the 'other' vis-à-vis modern and Western values and the European identity (Huysseune 2009, 66–68). The party was originally a pro-EU and anti-statist party, fighting for regional autonomy. However, during the 21st century, Lega has revealed a 'chameleonic logic' (Mazzoleni and Ruzza 2021, 69) and has changed its political and ideological discourse several times. Indeed, during the early 2000s, it shifted from a pro-EU to a Eurosceptic position and then, during Salvini's leadership, from regionalism to nationalism. These metamorphoses have progressively led Lega Nord towards the right-wing populist party's family, until its full ideological convergence in 2013 (Albertazzi et al. 2018; Tarchi 2015).

To explain Lega's shift scholars have focused on both internal and external causes. However, there is general consensus on the role played by the implementation of the EMU and its effects on the Italian economy. Engendering inflation and increasing both European and extra European external competition, EMU deepened the fear of globalisation among small and medium-sized entrepreneurs of Northern Italy. Therefore, Lega merged its traditional liberalism with new protectionist arguments as regional self-government and administrative autonomy was required to protect Northern Italians and the Northern economy from globalisation. The shift to Euroscepticism came from the perception that European institutions had progressively taken a dirigiste attitude. Hence, Lega extended its traditional anti-statist speech to European institutions. Euroscepticism did not entail a radical change in Lega's ideological base. It remained a populist and ethno-regionalist party, mainly focused on protecting of Northern Italy's interests (McDonnell 2006). Thus, the shift to Euroscepticism responds to a 'survival strategy' for maintaining its traditional electorate in the new political context. The modest results obtained by Lega at the national political elections of 2001 (3.94% in the House of Representatives), contrasting with the results of the previous election of 1996 (10.07% in the House of Representatives; 10.41 in the Senate) illustrates well the minority framework of Euroscepticism in Italy at the time. In addition, the Eurosceptic rhetoric brought Lega closer to the ideology of right-wing European parties. However, in this context, anti-EU feelings did not lead to any strategy of 'alliance' of right-wing populists at a supranational level. In a political context still dominated by mainstream media and a broad consensus on EMU, right-wing populist discourses were marginal.

Lega's second shift from regionalism to nationalism during Salvini's leadership, and the new political alliance strategy with European right-wing populist parties, also derived both from internal and external causes. Nevertheless, it is impossible to fully understand this move without considering the post-truth context. The financial crisis and the refugee crisis made the regionalist discourse irrelevant, since European austerity politics affected both Northern and Southern Italy. Secondly, the European migration crisis, mainly affecting Southern Italy, displaced the 'us' against the 'others' context. Thus, all Italian people were now menaced by migration influxes. The strengthening of both Eurosceptic and xenophobic feelings of the Italian people represented a chance to revitalise Lega. In this regard, the anti-European rhetoric became dominant in Salvini's discourse. On the one hand, European technocratic elites, acting to protect their financial interests, threatened the Italian people and the democratic roots of the West. On the other hand, European migration politics led to multicultural societies which could destroy both the Italian and the European identity. In sum, under Salvini's rhetoric, the European Union represented the most dangerous enemy of the Italian and the European people, enforcing a radical change in the party's political agenda. In the domestic sphere, people across Italy had to overcome their historical divisions to build a national opposition to European politics and to the influx of refugees (Albertazzi et al. 2018; Mazzoleni and Ruzza 2021, 69–75). Internationally, the party had to work on an alliance with right-wing populist parties in Europe.

Albertazzi et al. (2018) show how the use of social media has succeeded in ensuring a key disjunction between the leader and the party's politics, exemplified by the duplication of the party's names. Although the party's name remained Lega Nord, it has participated in the last electoral appointments with different names: 'Noi con Salvini' for the Italian local elections of 2017, and simply 'Lega' for the Italian general election of 2018 and the European election of 2019. This duplication of names reflects the deepest division in the party's politics. While in Northern Italy local leaders have continued to develop a regionalist and autonomist discourse, Salvini, through social media, has built his new nationalistic and xenophobic rhetoric – and it is fully grounded in a post-truth logic (Rowinski 2021, 121–141).

> Salvini's decision to heavily rely on social media – and his ability to do so effectively – also helps to explain why he could

bring about such a profound ideological shift so quickly, without relying on any intermediaries (Albertazzi Giovannini and Seddone 2018, 652).

Based on permanent visibility and inflammatory rhetoric, Salvini has enriched different 'hate speeches', not founded in facts, against his many enemies – 'clandestini' (illegal migrants), European institutions, political elites and the public opinion. Through the use of social media he has accomplished a complex and successful communicational strategy, exploiting the fears and feelings of the Italian people for his own electoral goals. Thanks to the use of an algorithmic software called 'La Bestia' (The Beast), Lega's communication team has succeeded in quickly analysing followers' reactions and feelings, adjusting and organising the party's strategy according to their followers' interests and wishes (Cervi 2020). The creation in 2015 of Facebook Live was a further advantage for Salvini. As Cervi points out, Salvini typically records streamed videos with his smartphone, often in familiar locations and in informal attire, allowing followers to express live reactions or to ask questions. The everyday language used by Salvini enhances the feeling of solidarity and the illusion of proximity, blurring the barriers between the public and private sphere and giving followers the perception of an intimate connection with the leader. In addition, anyone who criticises the leader is regarded as the 'other' – a member of the 'elite', not the 'people'. Rowinski calls such behaviour a 'blind faith' to the leader (Rowinski 2021, 28).

Rowinski (2021, 149–150) uses discursive historical analysis to unravel the narrative of populist Euroscepticism and emotive rhetoric. Both are present in Salvini's rhetoric under two main terms: 'Europa' and 'immigrazione'. Under 'Europa', Salvini is perceived as the one who makes Europe tremble, but he is also perceived as a populist and a xenophobe. In a post-truth logic, his followers do not seem to consider the latter characteristics as flaws. Instead, they focus on Salvini as a feared leader resisting the European elite and putting Italy first. The term 'immigrazione' relates to nativist messages that have reinforced populist forces through videos, pictures and short messages broadcast on social media. For instance, during the peak of the migrant crisis (while serving as Interior Minister) he denied the entrance of rescue ships in Italian ports. On social media, Salvini spread xenophobic propaganda filled with selective stories, not based on data, about the rise of criminality and unemployment due to the inflow of refugees and uncontrolled influxes of migrants (Bulli 2021). A quick look at Lega's two last electoral results in the national general elections highlights Salvini's political success under a post-truth strategy. Thus, while in the election of 2013 Lega obtained a modest 4.09% of votes in the House of Representatives and 4.34% in the Senate – by 2018 they had reached 17.35% in the Chamber of Representatives and 17.61% in the Senate – becoming a party government in coalition with Movement Five Stars.

At the international level, Matteo Salvini stated that while the term populist was used as an insult, for him it was a compliment (Mudde 2019, 5). Indeed, under Salvini's rhetoric, the European Union represented the most dangerous enemy of the Italian and European people, and the party had to work in an alliance with other right-wing populist parties in Europe. Thus, Salvini became, together with Marine Le Pen, the main promoter of the creation of 'an international group of nationalists' (McDonnell and Werner 2019, 155) in the European Parliament. He argued that an alliance of all European right-wingers and soft Eurosceptic parties should fight against the European globalist and multiculturalist elites on the transnational issues of migration, European welfare and European identity (McDonnell and Werner 2019; Martinelli 2018). As McDonnell and Werner (2019) point out, this statement reveals a new attitude in European right-wing populist parties– the use of social media allowed to veer towards an 'offensive' perspective, based on fake news, hate speech and a permanent condemnation of the dictatorship of the mainstream media (Froio and Ganesh 2019). Essentially, social media has enabled radical right-wing parties to become mainstreamed and normalised as part of the right-wing family of soft Eurosceptic parties, fighting to save the European people, the European democracy and European values (McDonnell and Werner 2019, 149–155). In the European Election of 2019, Lega obtained 34.33% of votes, while in previous elections they had reached a modest 6.16%. Hence, they became the first party in Italy to join the new 'Identity and Democracy' grouping in the European Parliament.

Post-truth logic allowed Salvini to build a new personal ideology that was based on the communicational potentialities of social media. By improving the illusion of a strong proximity to the people and of a direct dialogue with his supporters, Salvini succeeded in exploring the malaise of Italian society and the feelings of distrust on the European institution to reach unprecedent electoral successes both at a national and European level. Yet, Salvini's communicational strategy also entails an 'empty nationalism' (Albertazzi et al. 2018, 646), rooted in a contradictory discourse which is unable to respond to political challenges. Therefore, it is impossible to conceal Northern Italy's requests for administrative autonomy with the South's welfare needs – or even to simultaneously protect the state's autonomy and Europeanism. Salvini's fall from office post-2019 suggests that such post-truth logic may only result in a brief and ephemeral political success. However, it is important to consider this example as part of a wider reflection on the wider rise of populism throughout Europe.

Further remarks

In the post-truth age, right-wing populist parties such as Lega Nord offered an array of unrestrained 'truths' and managed to purposely distort problems and solutions in order to gain popularity and power. Lega's case in Italy has demonstrated that successive European crises have provided a competitive advantage for right-wing populism to grow. In turn, social media further empowered Lega's leaders to propagate their populist rhetoric with no filter and no accountability. As proven by Lega's electoral success, right-wing populism has succeeded, at least to an extent, in undermining the European integration project. Moving to the present, the Covid-19 pandemic seems to have ushered in a new sense of European solidarity, if still fragile. Collaboration between supranational institutions and the member states has succeeded in controlling the social effects arising from the pandemic, including developing a common European vaccination plan. Concurrently, the European Recovery Fund for a digital and ecological transition appears to have helped relaunch the European integration project. European solidarity over the Russian invasion of Ukraine is also noteworthy. Nonetheless, the European Union has multiple challenges to overcome in order to strengthen public trust and deepen the feeling of belonging amongst the European population. Although further work (and the passage of time) is required to disentangle these complexities, recent developments may form an opportunity to revitalise the European project (suitably tailored to valid social and democratic concerns) against the right-wing populism and post-truth rhetoric as explored in this chapter.

This study was conducted at the Research Center in Political Science (UIDB/CPO/00758/2020), University of Évora and supported by the Portuguese Foundation for Science and Technology (FCT) and the Portuguese Ministry of Education and Science through national funds.

References

BOOKS

Albertazzi, Daniele and Duncan McDonnell. 2015. *Populists in Power.* London-New-York: Routledge.

Bergmann, Eirikur. 2020. *Neo-Nationalism. The Rise of Nativist Populism.* Switzerland: Palgrave Macmillan.

Beyme, Klaus von. 1988. *Right-Wing Extremism in Western Europe.* London and New York: Routledge.

Cento Bull, Anna and Mark Gilbert. 2001. *The Lega Nord and the Northern Question in Italian Politics.* New York: Palgrave MacMillan.

Cosentino, Gabriele. 2020. Social Media and the Post-Truth World Order. New York: Palgrave MacMillan.

Dinan, Desmond, Nugent Neill and Paterson William. 2017. *The European Union in Crisis*. London: Palgrave MacMillan.

Heinisch, Reinhard, Massetti Emanuele and Mazzoleni Oscar (eds). 2019. *The People and the Nation Populism and Ethno-Territorial Politics in Europe*. New York: Routledge.

McDonnell, Duncan and Annika Werner. 2019. *International Populism. The radical right in the European Parliament.* New York: Oxford University Press.

McIntyre, Lee. 2018. Post-truth. Cambridge: MIT Press.

Mudde, Cas and Kaltwasser Cristóbal Rovira. 2017. *Populism: A Very Short Introduction*. Oxford University Press. Kindle Edition.

Mudde, Cas. *The Far Right Today*. UK: Polity Press.

Rowinsky, Paul. 2021. *Post-Truth, Post-Press, Post-Europe.* Euroscepticism and the Crisis of Political Communication. New York: Palgrave MacMillan. Kindle edition.

Tarchi, Marco. 2015. *Italia populista. Dal qualunquismo a Beppe Grillo.* Milano: Il Mulino.

Vasilopoulou, Sofia. 2018. *Far Right Parties and Euroscepticism: Patterns of Opposition*. Colchester: ECPR Press.

Torres, Francisco, Verdun Amy and Zimmermann Hubert. 2004. EMU Rules: The Political and Economic Consequences of European Monetary Integration. Internationale Politische Ökonomie. Baden-Baden: Nomos Verlagsgesellschaft mbH und Co.

Webber, Douglas. 2019. *European Disintegration? The Politics of Crisis in the European Union*. London: Red Globe Press.

BOOK CHAPTERS

Albertazzi, Daniele and Sean Mueller. 2017. 'Populism and liberal democracy: populists in government in Austria, Italy, Poland and Switzerland' in *The Populist Radical Right. A reader*, edited by Cas Mudde. London/New York: Routledge.

Bennett, W. Lance and Steven Livingston. 2021. 'A Brief History of the Disinformation Age. Information Wars and the Decline of Institutional Authority' in *The Disinformation Age. Politics, Technology, and Disruptive Communication in the United States,* edited by Lance Bennett and Steven Livingston. 3–40. Cambridge: Cambridge University Press.

Buonanno, Laurie. 2007. 'The European Migration Crisis' in *The European Union in Crisis* Diann, edited by Desmond Dinan, Neill Nugent and William Paterson. 100–130. London: Palgrave MacMillan.

Bulli, Giorgia. 2018. 'The populist representation of the people in the Italian *ius soli* political debate. The Lega Nord and the Movimento Cinque Stelle' in *Populism and the crisis of democracy*, edited by Gregor Fitzi, Jurgen Machert and Bryan S. Turner. 11–28. London/New York: Routledge.

Caiani, Manuela and Graziano Paolo. 2021. 'Understanding Varieties of Populism in Europe in Times of Crises' in *Varieties of Populism in Europe in Times of Crises,* edited by Manuela Caiani and Paolo Graziano, 1–18. Taylor and Francis.

Crawford, Beverly. 2021. 'Moral Leadership or Moral Hazard? Germany's Response to the Refugee Crisis and Its Impact on European Solidarity' in Riddervold Marianne, Trondal Jarle and Newsome Akasemi (eds). *The Palgrave Handbook of EU Crises.* 468–485. Palgrave Macmillan.

Froio, Caterina. 2021. 'Italy' in *Populism and New Patterns of Political Competition in Western Europe*, edited by Daniele Albertazzi and Davide Vampa. 250–268. London/New York: Routledge.

Kriesi, Hanspeter and Pappas Takis S. 2015. 'Populism in Europe During Crisis: An Introduction' in *Populism in the Shadow of the Great Recession*, edited by Hanspeter Kriesi and Takis S. Pappas, 343–345. Colchester: ECPR Press.

Lacey, Joseph and Nicolaïdis Joseph. 2020. 'Democracy and Disintegration: Does the "State of Democracy" in the EU Put the Integrity of the Union at Risk?' in *Governance and Politics in the Post-Crisis European Union*, edited by Ramona Coman, Amandine Crespy and Vivien A. Schmidt. 378–397. Cambridge: Cambridge University Press.

Martinelli, Alberto. 2018. 'Populism and Nationalism: The (Peculiar) Case of Italy' in *When Populism Meets Nationalism. Reflections on Parties in Power,* edited by Alberto Martinelli. 13–46. Milano: Ledizioni.

Mazzoleni, Oscar and Carlo Ruzza. 2021. 'Claiming regionalismo and nationalism at the same time: how Italian and Swiss Leagues can engage in contradictory claims and get away with it' in *The People and the Nation. Populism and Ethno-Territorial Politics in Europe,* edited by Reinhard Heinisch, Emanuele Massetti and Oscar Mazzoleni, 64–87. London/New York: Routledge.

McDonnell Duncan and Davide Vampa. 2016. 'The Italian Lega Nord' in *Understanding Populist Party Organization: The Radical Right in Western Europe*, edited by Reinhard Heinisch and Oscar Mazzoleni. 105–130. New York: Palgrave MacMillan.

Newsome, Akasemi, Riddervold Marianne and Trondal Jarle. 2021. 'The Legitimacy Crisis: An Introduction' in *The Palgrave Handbook of EU Crises*, edited by Riddervold Marianne, Trondal Jarle and Newsome Akasemi (eds). 595–602. Palgrave MacMillan.

Nunan Richard, Navin Mark Christopher. 2020. 'Introduction: Conceptualizing Populism, Democracy, and Truth'. In *Democracy, Populism, and Truth*, edited by Richard Nunan, Mark Christopher Navin, AMINTAPHIL: The Philosophical Foundations of Law and Justice, vol 9. Springer, Cham.

Schmidtke, Oliver. 2004. 'Politicising EMU: the "legitimacy gap" and the populist challenge to the EU' in *EMU Rules: The Political and Economic Consequences of European Monetary Integration*, edited by Francisco Torres, Amy Verdun and Hubert Zimmermann. 19–34. Internationale Politische Ökonomie. Baden-Baden: Nomos Verlagsgesellschaft mbH und Co.

Shapiro, Martin. 2021. 'The Perfect Storm'. In Riddervold Marianne, Trondal Jarle and Newsome Akasemi (eds). *The Palgrave Handbook of EU Crises,* 710–717. Palgrave Macmillan.

Taggart, Aleks and Paul Szczerbiak. 2008. 'Introduction: Researching Euroscepticism in European Party. A Comparative and Theoretical Research Agenda'. In *Opposing Europe? The Comparative Party Politics of Euroscepticism*, V.2, edited by Aleks Taggart and Paul Szczerbiak. 1–27. New York: Oxford University Press.

Tarchi, Marco. 2008. 'A Country of Many Populisms' in *Twenty-First Century Populism. The Spectre of Western European Democracy,* edited by Daniele Albertazzi and Duncan McDonnell, 84–99. New York: Palgrave MacMillan.

Tumber, Howard and Waisbord Silvio. 2021. 'Introduction' in *The Routledge Companion to Media Disinformation and Populism, edited by* Howard Tumber, and Silvio Waisbord, 1–12; 13–25. New York: Routledge.

Tumber, Howard and Waisbord Silvio. 2021. 'Media, disinformation, and populism. Problems and Responses'. In *The Routledge Companion to Media Disinformation and Populism, edited by* Howard Tumber, and Silvio Waisbord, 13–25. New York: Routledge.

ARTICLES AND RESEARCH PAPERS

Albertazzi, Daniele and Duncan McDonnell. 2005. 'The Lega Nord in the Second Berlusconi Government: A League of Its Own'. *Western European Politics* 28(5): 952–972.

Albertazzi, Daniele, Arianna Giovannini and Antonella Seddone. 2018. '"No regionalism please, we are Leghisti!" The transformation of the Italian Lega Nord under the leadership of Matteo Salvini'. *Regional & Federal Studies.* 288(5): 645–671.

Baume Maia de la. 2021. 'Orbán, Le Pen, Salvini join forces to blast EU integration'. *Politico.* https://www.politico.eu/article/viktor-orban-marine-le-pen-matteo-salvini-eu-integration-european-superstate-radical-forces/

Cervi, Laura. 2020. 'Veni, vidi, Facebooked-live: análisis del éxito de Matteo Salvini en Facebook'. *Revista CIDOB d'Afers Internacionals.* 124: 99–122.

Chiaramonte, Alessandro, De Sio Lorenzo and Vincenzo Emanuele. 2020. 'Salvini's success and the collapse of the Five-star Movement: The European elections of 2019'. *Contemporary Italian Politics* 12(2): 140–154.

Harsin, Jayson. 2015. 'Regimes of Posttruth, Postpolitics, and Attention Economies'. In *Communication, Culture & Critique,* 8(2): 327–333.

Hooghe, Liesbet and Marks Gary. 2019. 'Grand theories of European integration in the twenty-first century'. *Journal of European Public Policy.* 26(8). https://www.tandfonline.com/doi/full/10.1080/13501763.2019.1569711

Huysseune, Michel. 2010. 'A Eurosceptic vision in a Europhile country'. *Modern Italy* 15(1): 63–75.

Kopecky, Petr. and Mudde, Cas. (2002) "The Two Sides of Euroscepticism. Party Positions on European Integration in East Central Europe", *European Union Politics*, 3(3): 297–326.

Lehn, Stefan. 2017. "Populism: The Risks and Impact on European States. *International Affairs Forum*. https://carnegieeurope.eu/2017/06/06/populism-risks-and-impact-on-european-states-pub-71170

McDonnell, Duncan. 2006. 'A Weekend in Padania: Regionalist Populism and the Lega Nord'. In *Politics* 26(2): 126–132.

Negri, Fedra, Nicoli Francesco and Kuhn Theresa. 2020. "Common currency, common identity? The impact of the Euro introduction on European identity". *European Union Politics*, 22: 114–132.

Vasilopolou, Sofia. 2009. 'Varieties of Euroscepticism: The Case of the European Extreme Right'. *Journal of Contemporary European Research*, 5(1): 3-23.

Waisbord, Silvio. 2018. "The Elective Affinity Between Post-Truth Communication and Populist Politics." *Communication Research and Practice* 4: 7–34. https://doi.org/10.1080/22041451.2018.1428928

Wassenberg, Birte. 2020. 'Challenging the origins of Euroscepticism. A historical perspective'. *Historia y Política*, 44: 55–79.

Westlake, Martin. 2019. 'The more (European integration) there is, the more (Euroscepticism) there is: Euroscepticism as reactive identity formation and the importance of opposition. Where might the EU institutions go from here?' *Bruges Political Research Papers*, 73. https://core.ac.uk/reader/200288653

7

Postcolonial Gaslighting and Greenland: When Post-Truth Gets in the Way of Independence

EMIL SONDAJ HANSEN

The starting point for Aki-Maltida Høegh-Dam is the tired myth that Greenland throughout all the years was a Danish colony just like Hans Egede was a 'cruel colonizer'. The claim does not become more true by being repeated
– Katrine Winkel Holm.

When deciding what a colony is, it is often assumed that one can look to international law for a definitive answer. Others finds the definition directly measurable from the level of extracted natural resources determining the colonial status. The case of Greenland's independence struggle shows that determining what a colony is much more complex and can take place in a realm where discourse is determined more by emotion, belief and distortion than by facts – to borrow the definition of post-truth given by the Oxford English Dictionary in 2016. After achieving 'Home Rule' in 1979, the Greenlandic government achieved 'Self-Rule' in 2009, allowing the island to declare independence from Denmark, should it want to. With an electoral majority for independence, and with Denmark concerned about its reputation as a 'model citizen' of international society (Sharman 2013, 190), something appears to be delaying the prospect of independence. This chapter proposes the theoretical concept of postcolonial gaslighting to make sense of this puzzle and analyse subtle and implicit forms of colonialism and domination. Postcolonial gaslighting captures a variety of techniques and mechanisms to make one doubt a particular version of reality and subsequently be chastised for being responsible for one's circumstances. The argument is that the debate about independence consists of competing conceptions of reality and understandings of concepts grounded in emotion and belief, that is, operating in a post-truth manner. When there is no objective way to resolve competing claims about the inherent value of independence or the extent of Danish postcolonial responsibility, the competing claims must be resolved in a different way. The concept of postcolonial gaslighting shows that one vision of reality is portrayed as less legitimate than the other. This destabilising challenge to Greenlandic experiences of the reality of the relationship contributes to ontological insecurity and prevents agentic action to be taken towards the realisation of independence. The past structures the future possibilities, so when the past is challenged in the realm of post-truth, it limits the scope of future action. The chapter thus shows that the effects of post-truth can prolong hierarchical relationships in global politics by using Greenland as a case study.

I analyse competing visions of the relationship between Denmark and Greenland by drawing on two exchanges in the Danish parliament. The format of the debate provides a means of analysing competing visions and highlights the tension between these in a formalised setting. After outlining the concept of postcolonial gaslighting and its relation to the ontological security literature, I examine the exchange between Greenlandic MP Aki-Matilda Høegh-Dam and Danish MP Morten Messerschmidt at the opening parliamentary debate in 2019. This exchange illustrates how accounts of Greenland's colonial past are denied and dismissed through invoking gendered stereotypes. I then examine the competing visions underpinning this exchange about what a colony is by looking at the reactions to Høegh-Dam's speech in the Danish media. This shows that there are two competing visions of reality, but one is portrayed as more legitimate through the tools of postcolonial gaslighting. The next section examines an exchange between former Greenlandic prime minister Aleqa Hammond and former Danish prime minister Lars Løkke Rasmussen about hidden American military activities in Greenland. This highlights how the debate about independence consists of two competing visions of the value of independence, one highlighting material factors and one privileging the intrinsic worth of independence for postcolonial peoples. One vision is however portrayed as less legitimate through the deployment of stereotypes of Greenlandic incompetency. The last section examines how postcolonial gaslighting allows Danish elites to blame Greenland for the failure to live up to the criteria of statehood.

Postcolonial gaslighting and ontological insecurity

Key to my understanding of post-truth is competition and struggle over truth claims without any legitimate arbiter to adjudicate such competing claims. Rather than exclusively denoting Trumpian-styled lying, I find the concept of post-truth a helpful framework for making sense of the political effects of clashes between two competing experiences of reality. As Bailey points out, there is no 'epistemic terra firma' (2020, 667), so epistemology and knowledge are always political and subject to contestation. Post-truth as an analytic frame thereby foregrounds epistemic competition, which according to Sismondo, 'is as much about choosing which truths can be considered salient and important as about which claims can be considered true and false' (2017: 4). Such choices have important effects, as they in Fuller's terms 'epitomize the struggle for "modal power"', that is 'control over what is possible' (2018, 8).

These struggles in the realm of post-truth are not always fought innocently, and the Oxford English Dictionary's emphasis on distortion is key here. Danish elites actively distort Greenlandic experiences of the relationship through postcolonial gaslighting. Drawing on psychological and sociological work on gaslighting, I highlight how the mechanisms of postcolonial gaslighting destabilise perceptions of reality and thereby impede agency. Important work has been done on gaslighting in sociology (Sweet 2019), and the concept has achieved attention in the Trump years regarding disinformation (Stern 2018), but it has yet to be utilised in IR. Stern notes that gaslighting requires a level of intimacy between the abuser and abused (2018). The case of Denmark and Greenland is therefore appropriate, given the supposed intimacy of the Community of the Realm (The term describing Denmark, the Faroe Islands and Greenland) evidenced by the repeated use of family metaphors by Danish politicians to describe the relation between Denmark and Greenland (Gad 2008).

Disaggregating the concept, gaslighting has three main effects:

1. causing someone to doubt the validity of one's beliefs, thoughts and feelings
2. making someone feel confused or anxious
3. distorting one's sense of reality, ultimately with the effect of achieving control over someone. It falls short of being explicitly coercive, but rather consists of 'small strategies of control and confusion' (Sweet 2019, 862).

It is exercised through specific processes identified via the following levels:

- Withholding and refusing to engage in a conversation about certain things.
- Trivialising, belittling and disregarding someone's feelings and beliefs.
- Diverting and removing focus and challenging the credibility of the person.
- Invoking stereotypes, particularly racialised and gendered, to delegitimise the victim's account of reality.
- Denial or offering an alternative account, that directly contradicts the

victim's experience of reality. The invoking of stereotypes illustrates the incentive to push a struggle into the realm of post-truth for those with power in gendered and racialised hierarchies.

I conceptualise it as a distinct kind of 'postcolonial' gaslighting since it concerns the nature of Greenland's colonial status. It is important that I do not use the term 'postcolonial' as a periodisation implying that colonialism is a thing of the past that has now been transcended and overcome. On the contrary, I agree with Seth (2011, 174) that the term 'postcolonial' 'signifies the claim that conquest, colonialism and empire are not a footnote or episode in a larger story ... but are in fact a central part of that story and are constitutive of it'.

To examine the effects of this, I draw on the theoretical framework of ontological security. Ontological security is a way of making sense of how different experiences of truth impede agency, as the theoretical branch recognises that feelings of security are not always material. First coined by Laing, ontological security was then picked up by Giddens and later introduced to IR by Huysmans, spurring a wide-reaching literature. Huysmans (1998, 242) defined ontological security as a 'strategy of managing the limits of reflexivity – death as the undetermined – by fixing social relations into a symbolic and institutional order' with the purpose of 'making life intelligible'. The term essentially describes the security 'not of the body, but of the self' (Mitzen 2006, 344). The key assumption is that states, and crucially other units in the international system, desire a 'consistent sense of self' (Zarakol 2010, 3) based upon the basic need to experience oneself as a continuous entity in time (Mitzen 2006, 342). Steele (2008), for instance, explains why Belgium decided to fight against Germany during the Second World War, despite having no chance of success by reference to the desire for a consistent autobiographical narrative of bravery.

Key to the argument of this chapter is ontological security's emphasis on agency. Mitzen (2006, 344) highlights how a subjective sense of the self is what 'enables and motivates action and choice'. Subotic and Zarakol (2012, 917) further argue that 'agency is not possible without a concept of the self'. Agency requires a clear continuous understanding of the self's past, present and future. I argue that the contestation over the 'truth' of the colonial status of Greenland through postcolonial gaslighting contributes to ontological insecurity and anxiety, preventing Greenlandic elites exercising agency to allow independence to materialise. The case of Greenland diverges from the cases discussed in the established literature of ontological security. Firstly, the literature discusses relatively bounded and established entities, namely states. Greenland offers a different kind of challenge, since it is transitional – on the path to statehood. The ontological security needs of Greenland are therefore complicated since the very ontological status of Greenland is in flux. In this sense, I embrace Yu Untalan's call for a postcolonial approach to ontological security that avoids the 'normalizing logics of the Westphalian nation-state system' (2019, 43). Yu Untalan takes issue with the self-regarding nature of ontological security literature, that has seen the Other as a source of insecurity, rather than a possible source of ontological security. However, I argue that a first step to achieving the 'creative, non-destructive ways of confronting ontological insecurities' that Yu Untalan calls for and to view 'the postcolonial Other as a learning source for the Self' is to properly expose and understand the mechanisms of distortion and power currently at play in the relationship between Denmark and Greenland (2019, 40).

These mechanisms of distortion have largely been absent from the established ontological security literature. The gaslighting metaphor thus fills an important gap in the literature by introducing such mechanisms of contestation and distortion to feelings of ontological insecurity. It works well within the ontological security framework, as it highlights how barriers to agency can be deliberately constructed. It contributes to ontological insecurity by destabilising realities (Sweet 2019, 855) and preventing the stable sense of Self that is necessary for agency.

The indigenous Miss Denmark

This section offers empirical illustrations of the contestation over Greenland's colonial status, and shows how postcolonial gaslighting works in practice. I present the case of Aki-Matilda Høegh-Dam, a young Greenlandic MP who called for an open discussion of Greenland's colonial past, only to be met by fierce resistance from Danish politicians and public intellectuals. On this basis, I probe the different worldviews and conceptions of colonialism that underpin the tension between Høegh-Dam and her challengers to show how they are grounded in different conceptions of reality, that is, operating according to post-truth logics. When Aki-Matilda Høegh-Dam was elected to the Danish parliament for the Greenlandic party, Siumut in June 2019, she took the debate about Greenland's colonial past to an intensity not seen since prime minister Aleqa Hammond's calls for a reconciliation commission in 2014. Aged just 22, she stood as an impressive figure in the ceremonial opening debate of the Danish parliament, opening the lid on a Danish colonial past in her first speech as an elected representative:

> I as a young Greenlander and now as an MP experience the lag of the colonial era. We are for better or worse a product of the colonial era. Because, even though it was not me who was stateless like my brother's father, when he was born, and even though it was me who was part of the first cohort not to go

segregated schools like my parents, my siblings, yes, my entire family, I have still grown up with the lasting effects of the colonial era. No matter how much you deny the past, it still shapes our future (Folketinget 2019).

She argued that common trust between Denmark and Greenland rests upon a 'recognition of our common past' (Folketinget 2019). This trust was crucial for 'the ones who have experienced being hurt by the colonial mentality, through damage to family relations, increased violence, alcohol and substance abuse, that unfortunately has been brought on to next generations, to us' (Folketinget 2019).

Morten Messerschmidt from the Danish People's Party (DPP), a popular figure who still holds the record for most personal votes at a European Parliamentary election in Denmark, made two comments in response that represent the crux of postcolonial gaslighting:

> I am certain that Ms. Høegh-Dam knows the old Kierkegaard quotation: that life can only be understood backwards, but it must be lived forwards. And this is how it is often is with a country's, with a people's history: When you look back with the glasses of the present, there have been mistakes and unreasonableness. This is the case for women, who first received the right to vote in 1907 for municipal elections and in 1915 for parliamentary elections; for religious minorities who in Denmark just after the end of the Middle Ages also did not have the same privileges as Christians. So there are injustices that we will not repeat today. (Folketinget 2019).

Here we see several patterns of postcolonial gaslighting. It is noteworthy that Messerschmidt sees the need to first rebuke Høegh-Dam with an old Kierkegaard quotation, asserting that she surely must be familiar with one of the most important Danish philosophers, implicitly questioning whether or not she in fact is. There is also an element of trivialising the colonial experience by juxtaposing it with all other past injustices. This temporal move, that clearly separates the colonial from the postcolonial period, clearly denies the possibility of Høegh-Dam's subjective experience of the lasting effects of the 'colonial mentality'. Messerschmidt then proceeds:

> But what I don't understand about Ms. Høegh-Dam's speech is why she is using the past to deprive future generations of Greenlanders the privileges, that she herself has enjoyed. As I understand it, Ms. Høegh-Dam is born in Hillerød, has studied at the University of Copenhagen, has competed in a

competition by the name of Miss Denmark, that is, enjoyed that which is Denmark. If Ms. Høegh-Dam, is incarnated about wanting Greenlandic independence, how can that be compatible with the fact that she has enjoyed the fruits that is Denmark? And why can that generation, which she shall put into the world, and the generations thereafter, also not enjoy these same fruits?

Messerschmidt draws on Høegh-Dam's gender here to delegitimise her account of the relationship between Denmark and Greenland, and the colonial past. He insinuates that her account of the colonial past and her desire for independence is less valid, because she has competed in Miss Denmark. This is a clear attempt to divert focus by challenging the credibility of Høegh-Dam. He also takes a step further by linking Høegh-Dam's womanhood and reproductive capability to her opinions about independence. Assuming that her capacity for 'putting generations into the world' demands a certain responsibility about the future of Greenland that necessitates staying in the relationship with Denmark, and thereby requires a different presentation of the past than Høegh-Dam presents. This brings to mind abusers asking partners to stay in an unhealthy relationship for the sake of the children.

He also seeks to delegitimise her representativeness as a voice of Greenland by highlighting her relationship to Denmark, thus undermining her claim to be an indigenous Inuit. Strandsbjerg notes that Greenlandic identity consists of a territorially bounded political identity, and an ethnically defined Inuit identity (2014, 264). The indigenous foundations of Greenlandic identity are often largely dismissed with the former finance minister and president of the United Nations General Assembly, Mogens Lykketoft, going so far as to say that 'there are no longer any full-blooded Eskimos left in Greenland' (Breum 2014, 35). It also has to be noted that the word 'Greenland' in fact has no root in the Inuit language (Kleist 2004, 114). So, when Høegh-Dam in her speech at the opening parliamentary debate, used the Inuit name 'Kalaallit Nunaat' meaning 'Land of the Greenlandic Inuit' (Folketinget 2020, 20), she participated in a broader debate about the indigenous aspect of Greenland's identity.

The exchange between Høegh-Dam and Messerschmidt represents a case where two different conceptions of reality clash. It also mounts to a case of post-truth, since the validity of the accounts are not reconciled through any objective or agreed-upon metric, but rather rests upon emotions and feelings. However, these emotions are manipulated and contested by the deployment of the 'small strategies of control and confusion' of gaslighting (Sweet 2019, 862)

This case of postcolonial gaslighting is grounded in two different conceptions of what a colony is and thereby the standard by which to measure the past. Høegh-Dam's account of the colonial effects prompted fierce reactions. Public intellectual and theologian Katrine Winkel Holm accused Høegh-Dam of 'distorting Greenland's past' (2020). She took issue with Høegh-Dam's characterisation of the 'evil Danes that cold-heartedly exploited the Greenlanders', instead arguing that past Greenlanders were themselves 'the most eager advocates of the complete opening towards Denmark' (Winkel Holm 2020). Examining the motivations behind the 1953 incorporation and the practice of the referendum reveals a different picture. It is widely agreed that Denmark incorporated Greenland as a region to prevent the UN from supervising its decolonisation (Janussen 2019, 12) in a referendum that Greenlanders themselves did not participate in (Gad 2020, 34). Winkel Holm proceeds to argue that 'the starting point for Aki-Maltida Høegh-Dam is the tired myth that Greenland throughout all the years was a Danish colony just like Hans Egede was a 'cruel colonizer. The claim does not become more true by being repeated' (2020). She backs this up with the claim that the 'indigenous population in Greenland was not the Inuits, but the Norse who arrived in the 900s' (Winkel Holm 2020).

The intellectual ammunition for this argument is supplied by historian Thorkild Kjærgaard. Kjærgaard denies that Greenland was ever a colony, claiming that the Norse arrived in Greenland at the end of the 900s and were there before the Inuit, whom he labels an 'invasive people' (Kjærgaard 2019, 139). For Kjærgaard, Danish sovereignty over Greenland was thus never broken and Greenland has thereby never been colonised (Breum 2018, 41). He instead refers to Greenland as a 'Nordic sister-nation' (Kjærgaard 2021) to avoid the 'deluge of negative connotations' brought about by the 'colonial paradigm' (Kjærgaard 2019, 141, 149). Note here the depoliticising effects of presenting Greenland in gendered terms as a sister, implying a certain kind of equality. This conception of colonialism is grounded in a particular emphasis on sovereignty, but the idea of the 'negative connotations', implies that asserting what a colony is must be a comparative issue. Conservative MP Rasmus Jarlov more explicitly embraces this comparative focus in his rejection of Greenlandic colonial status by claiming that it is 'debatable' whether Greenland was a colony (Jørgensen and Stampe 2019). He argues that Greenland has not been sufficiently oppressed to qualify as a colony. Pushed by journalists on the validity of his statement, Jarlov refuses to be situated in the post-truth realm, by asserting that he builds his claim on 'facts, based on where Greenland's geographical location is... It was an area that was within Denmark-Norway's natural sphere of activity, and therefore I do not believe that it fits within the definition of a colony' (Jørgensen and Stampe 2019). The naturalisation of power and influence as a replacement of colonial status is noteworthy. He proceeds to argue that the colonial term, 'comes with misleading associations in relation to Greenlandic history. It gives an impression that Greenland has been oppressed to a degree which is not true' (Jørgensen and Stampe 2019). This allows him to later argue that it is in fact 'Denmark's merit that Greenland can even speak about independence today' (Jarlov 2021).

There are thus two competing visions of what it means to be a colony at play here. For Høegh-Dam it is a feeling and a mentality that transcends any specific periodisation of 'post' colonial times. For the Danish elites examined in this section, colonialism is in essence, something other states do. Wrapped up in explanations of Norse sovereignty, the explanation boils down to Greenland not being sufficiently oppressed to qualify as a colony amongst other colonies of the world. The tension between accepting postcolonial responsibility and Danish ontological security based on the identity as a 'model citizen of international society' (Sharman 2013, 190) prevents any serious attempt at reconciling these different accounts of the colonial history. Instead Høegh-Dam's account is trivialised and discarded through post-colonial gaslighting.

A tale of two prime ministers: The value of independence and the room of confidentiality

Just as the definition of a colony is contested through postcolonial gaslighting, so is the value of independence. An exchange between former Greenlandic Prime Minister Aleqa Hammond and former Danish Prime Minister Lars Løkke Rasmussen illustrates not only how Greenlandic feelings of injustice are dismissed through the mechanisms of postcolonial gaslighting, but also how discussions of independence operate with contradictory and contrasting visions of the value of independence. Aleqa Hammond did more than any other prime minister to bring the issue of the colonial past to the fore. In her 2014 New Year's speech, she called for a reconciliation commission and argued that reconciliation with painful taboos was necessary for citizens to 'take the power over their own life and contribute positively to society' (Hammond 2014, 8). Here, a lack of clarity about the past stands in the way of exercising agency over the future. It is thus not possible to achieve a continuous experience of the Self if the past traumas are unresolved. Yet, Danish elites have not accommodated this wish for clarity about the past. They have met it by withholding and a refusal to enter a conversation. Former Danish Prime Minister Helle Thorning Schmidt rejected the proposed reconciliation commission in 2014, reasoning that there was nothing to be reconciled (Breum 2018, 109).

While representing her party, Siumut in the Danish Parliament, Aleqa Hammond asked former Danish Prime Minister Lars Løkke Rasmussen about the responsibility for cleaning the radioactive waste left by Americans at Camp Century in Greenland. She highlighted the painful memories of the colonial past where Denmark did not inform Greenland of American nuclear activities on Greenlandic soil (Folketinget 2018a). Rasmussen responded: 'I cannot take away from Ms. Hammond, if Ms. Hammond thinks that there has been a series of unfortunate events' proceeding to highlight the economic benefits of American presence in Greenland (Folketinget 2018a). It is interesting here how Rasmussen does not deny Hammond's experience of history, yet he does not accept nor embrace it. He simply juxtaposes her experience with the economic benefits of an American presence.

This exchange highlights how Hammond and Rasmussen operate with two different conceptions of what independence means. In the interaction, Rasmussen does not recognise or embrace the Greenlandic sense of injustice but instead portrays it as something that can be directly measured against material benefits. Rasmussen is then implicitly operating with the same conflation of self-determination and material provisions, as Rezvani in his study of non-sovereignty: 'Full independence is therefore not the ultimate fulfilment of national self-determination if it does not fulfil a population's economic, political, and security self-interest' (2014, 4–5). Former Danish finance minister, Claus Hjort Frederiksen, articulates this vision as follows: 'If you do not have your economy in order, what is your independence then really, if you have to go around with your hat and get funding all the time' (Turnowsky 2019b). In contrast, Hammond's vision of self-determination and independence is more akin to Inayatullah's observation that sovereignty has a distinct value of its own that transcends material concerns, particularly for formerly colonised people (1996, 73). Former Greenlandic prime minister Kim Kielsen echoed this when he claimed that 'independence is not only about economy. Independence is also about identity and freedom' (2018, 1).

This second vision of independence is not often taken seriously but instead dismissed through postcolonial gaslighting. Hammond asked Rasmussen whether 'Denmark is ready to take on the full responsibility for the cleaning after military activities in Greenland, in light of the UN's human rights report on Greenland?' (Folketinget 2018b) – specifically referring to the radioactive waste at Camp Century, mentioned by a UN special rapporteur. Rasmussen responded by highlighting that the UN rapporteur had been approached by a minister in the Greenlandic government who subsequently had to step down and the request had been withdrawn (Folketinget 2018b). Rasmussen thereby deflected the potential postcolonial embarrassment that surrounds the question of American military activity (Olesen 2018) by drawing on the stereotype of incompetency and scandal in domestic Greenlandic politics. This is the gaslighting trick of invoking stereotypes to delegitimise a person's account of reality. Yet there is no *a priori* connection between Denmark's past actions and scandals in Greenlandic politics. By making such a connection,

Rasmussen perpetuates the discursive image of an incompetent Greenland that needs the competent Denmark to manage its affairs. Hammond further challenged Rasmussen on how Greenland has historically been in the dark about American affairs, most notably nuclear activities, saying that 'it is a very limited knowledge, we in Greenland have about the American's presence in our country' (Folketinget 2018b). Rasmussen again deflects through the language of competence. He argues that Hammond's point is why 'I spend a lot of energy on ... how we can create this room of confidentiality, which has to be there, if we are to handle some of these questions that Ms. Aleqa Hammond is raising here' (Folketinget 2018b). Here, Rasmussen insinuates that Greenlandic politicians in the past have been unable to conduct themselves in a manner appropriate for this 'room of confidentiality'. Involvement in Danish foreign policy regarding American activities on Greenland apparently has to be deserved. The logic behind this 'room of confidentiality' is similar to that of Greenland's independence more generally. Entrance into the society of states is conditional, and as Bartelsson points out, sovereignty has developed into something 'granted, contingent upon its responsible exercise' (2014, 1). By portraying Greenlandic politicians as incompetent and incapable of managing Greenland's affairs, Danish elites limit the possibility of Greenland living up to this responsible exercise.

Playing the Blame Game

Gaslighting does not only involve making the victim doubt its conception of reality. It also entails blaming the victim for this confusion. In her study of gaslighting victims, Sweet notes that abusers would construct a particular reality and then chastise the victim for the conditions to remove their autonomy (2019, 868). This captures the function of the postcolonial gaslighting. By delegitimising and removing focus from the Danish colonial responsibility, Danish elites are able to conceptually separate discussions about a future independent Greenland from questions of the colonial legacy. This blaming takes place particularly when the debate turns to the economy. The major argument is that Greenland is not sufficiently developed to be free of the annual Danish block grant of approximately 3.6 billion crowns. This narrows the debate about possible political alternatives to dependence on Denmark, anchored in a conception of sovereignty as capacity, echoing Jackson's analysis of 'quasi-states' (1990). While there are genuine challenges to be addressed on the path towards independence, the conversation about economic development is discursively separated from the colonial foundations of Greenland's contemporary problems. The emphasis on economic capacity must thus be seen in relation to the refusal to recognise Greenland's colonial past and the destabilising challenges to its postcolonial identity. The 'gaslighting' metaphor thus captures how Greenland is often chastised for failing to live up to certain criteria for statehood.

When asked about the dependency on the block grant, Aleqa Hammond responded 'we did not ask Demark to colonise us and come here to plant the flag. But what about the damn 3.6 billion crowns? Can we not just develop something ourselves? Yes, but it is not quite as easy' (Jensen 2013). However, Danish politicians do not take this historical dimension of Greenland's problems into account when drawing on metaphors of greedy teenagers (Gad 2008) and portraying the block grant as a prize to be won. Hammond argued that 'we still do too much harm to ourselves if we are to compare ourselves to other non-colonised people' (2013, 19) highlighting the implied inferiority present in Danish discussions of economic independence. Former Greenlandic Prime Minister Hans Enoksen previously challenged these constructed barriers to independence, declaring that 'we are neither blind nor in denial towards our problems – our social issues shall not be a hindrance to the development of our self-determination' (2007, 2).

The move of blaming Greenland for its own problems allows Danish politicians to reject any future support for an independent Greenland. Denmark has historically been one of the most generous donors of foreign aid in the world – would it not be appropriate to support and provide aid to its former colony?   When asked about financially supporting an independent Greenland, former foreign minister Martin Lidegaard responded that Danish financial support post-independence would not be 'fair or an expression of mutual respect' (Breum 2018, 55). This highlights that debates about the colonial past have very real effects in how they structure future possibilities. In Fuller's terms, the debate about the colonial past is thus a struggle for modal power – 'control over what is possible' (2018, 8).

Conclusion: Post-truth and polarisation

This chapter has shown that the framework of post-truth allows us to make sense of the debate about Greenland's colonial past and its possible future. The challenges to Greenland's autobiographical self, in terms of its colonial past, destabilises perceptions of reality and prevent the possibility of agency in the future. The theoretical tool of postcolonial gaslighting shows how contested realities in the realm of post-truth are distorted and manipulated by Danish elites. The problem is not so much that there are entirely different understandings of reality. The problem is that one is presented as more legitimate than the other through the subtle strategies of coercion inherent in postcolonial gaslighting. We have seen how Høegh-Dam's account of the colonial mentality was dismissed through gendered stereotypes. Hammond's challenge to being left in the dark about American military activities in Greenland was rejected based on stereotypes of incompetency. Rejecting the colonial experience ultimately provides the conceptual foundations for putting the blame for the current issues and obstacles on the path towards statehood with the Greenlandic people.

Post-truth and postcolonial gaslighting allow us to make sense of subtle forms of colonialism in the contemporary era. But what are the effects of such post-truth discussions of the colonial past? Staying clear of any clear-cut predictions, there are signs that the debate is becoming increasingly polarised. Pele Broberg was forced to step down as Greenlandic Foreign Minister in September 2021 after declaring that only those with Inuit heritage should be able to vote in a referendum about Greenland's future (Brøns 2021). When the discussion on colonial heritage is being held in the realm of post-truth and postcolonial gaslighting, such quasi-racialised demarcations are allowed to emerge through frustrations about the lack of recognition of the reality of Greenland's colonial past. The Greenlandic national anthem reads – Impossibly now to remain calm; Kalaallit, towards great goals we embark, As freeborn people we will in the country live; Begin to believe in your own abilities (Højskolesangbogen 2021). Suspended in the transition towards statehood, Greenland is unable to remain calm. Its ontological insecurities prevent agency. Trapped between Danish efforts to neglect the colonial past and its postcolonial burden. Yet still, the desire for independence continues. Kalaallit Nunaat continues on the path towards 'great goals' – perhaps indefinitely.

References

Bailey, A. 2020. 'Gaslighting and Epistemic Harm: Editor's Introduction' *Hypatia* 35(4), 667–673.

Bartelson, J. 2014. *Sovereignty as symbolic form, Critical issues in global politics*. New York: Routledge.

Breum, M. 2018. *Hvis Grønland river sig løs.* Copenhagen: Gyldendal.

Breum, M. 2014. *Balladen om Grønland: Trangen til løsrivelse, råstofferne og Danmarks dilemma*. Copenhagen: Gyldendal.

Brøns, M. 2021. 'Pele Broberg er ikke længere naalakkersuisoq for udenrigsanliggender'. 27/09/2021. *KNR*. Available at: https://knr.gl/da/nyheder/pele-broberg-er-ikke-længere-naalakkersuisoq-udenrigsanliggender

noksen, H. 2007. *Landsstyreformand Hans Enoksens åbningstale.* Available at https://naalakkersuisut.gl/~/media/Nanoq/Files/Attached%20Files/Taler/DK/aabnings taler/aabningstale_EM_2007_HE_DK.pdf

Folketinget, 2020. *3rd Meeting (Opening Debate of the Danish Parliament)* 08/10/2020. Available at: https://www.ft.dk/ forhandlinger/20201/20201M003_2020-10-08_0900.htm

Folketinget, 2019. *3rd Meeting (Opening Debate of the Danish Parliament)* 03/10/2019. Available at: https://www.ft.dk/ forhandlinger/20191/20191M003_2019-10-03_1000.htm

Folketinget, 2018a. § 20-spørgsmål US 2 Om *Arktis og om lufthavne i Grønland.* 13/11/2018. Available at: https://www.ft.dk/samling/20181/ spoergsmaal/us2/index.htm

Folketinget, 2018b. § 20-spørgsmål US 16 Om *Thulebasen.* 11/12/2018. Available at: https://www.ft.dk/samling/20181/spoergsmaal/US16/index. htm#t99B59D5055A248B38E52626BF2FDF907tab1

Fuller, S. 2018: *Post-truth: Knowledge As A Power Game.* London: Anthem Press.

Gad, U.P. 2020. 'Greenland, the Faroe Islands, and Denmark', in: Christiansen, P.M., Elklit, J. and Nedergaard, P. (Eds.), *The Oxford Handbook of Danish Politics.* Oxford: Oxford University Press, pp.29–45. Gad, U.P., 2008. 'Når mor/barn-relationen bliver teenager: Kompatible rigsfællesskabsbilledersom (dis)integrationsteori.' *Politica - Tidsskrift for Politisk Videnskab* 40(2): 111–133.

Hammond, A. 2014. *Nytårstale 2014 Aleqa Hammond, Formand for Naalakkersuisut* Available at: https://naalakkersuisut.gl/~/media/Nanoq/Files/ Attached%20Files/Taler/DK/Nytaarst ale%202014.pdf

Hammond, A. 2013. *Åbningstale ved Formand for Naalakkersuisut, Aleqa Hammond* Available at https://naalakkersuisut.gl/~/media/Nanoq/Files/ Attached%20Files/Taler/DK/aabnings_taler/Talen%202013%20EM%20 med%20skabelon.pdf

Hersher, R. 2016. 'The Arctic Suicides: It's Not The Dark That Kills You'. 21/04/2016. *NPR.* Available at https://www.npr.org/sections/ goatsandsoda/2016/04/21/474847921/the-arctic-suicides-its-not-the-dark- that-kills-you

Huysmans, J. 1998. 'Security! What Do You Mean? From Concept to Thick Signifier'. *European Journal of International Relations.* 4(2): 226–255.

Højskolesangbogen, 2021. 'Nunarput utoqqarsuanngoravit'. Available at: https://www.hojskolesangbogen.dk/om-sangbogen/historier-om-sangene/m-n/nunarput-utoqqarsuanngoravit-vort-aeldgamle-land/

Inayatullah, N.1996. 'Beyond the Sovereignty Dilemma: Quasi-States as Social Construct' in: Biersteker, T.J. and Weber, C. (Eds.), *State Sovereignty as Social Construct.* Cambridge: Cambridge University Press, pp. 50–80.

Jackson, R.H. 1990. *Quasi-states: sovereignty, international relations, and the Third World*, Cambridge: Cambridge University Press.

Janussen, J. 2019. 'Grønlands vej til større selvbestemmelsesret: Muligheder og begrænsninger i juridiske, administrative og andre perspektiver'. *Politik* 22 (1): 11–27.

Jarlov, R. 2021. 'Uden Danmark havde Grønland været langt mindre frit, end det er i dag'. 21/09/2021. *Berlingske*. Available at https://www.berlingske.dk/kommentarer/uden-danmark-havde-groenland-vaeret-langt-mindre-frit-end-det-er-i-dag

Jensen, C. 2013. 'Nultolerance, brun sovs og hvalbøffer'. *Information* 18/03/2013. Available at: https://www.information.dk/udland/2013/11/nultolerance-brun-sovs-hvalboeffer

Jørgensen, V.L. and Stampe, C. 2019. 'Detektor: Grønland var altsa° en dansk koloni, Rasmus Jarlov'. *DR* 24/08/2019 Available at: https://www.dr.dk/nyheder/detektor/detektor-groenland-var-altsaa-en-dansk-koloni-rasmus-jarlov

Kielsen, K. 2018. Fællesskab *og solidaritet Nytårstale af Formanden for Naalakkersuisut Kim Kielsen.* Available at: https://naalakkersuisut.gl/~/media/Nanoq/Files/Attached%20Files/Taler/DK/Nytaarst

Kjærgaard, T. 2021. *Biografi.* Available at: https://thorkildkjaergaard.com/biografi/

Kjærgaard, T. 2019. 'Kolonihistorie uden koloni: Om Grønlandsbindet i den Nye Danske Kolonihistorie'. *Temp - Tidsskrift for Historie* 9 (17): 138–144.

Kleist, M. 2004. 'The Status of the Greenlandic Inuit. Are the Greenlandic Inuit a People, an Indigenous People, a Minority, or a Nation? A Practical, Philosophical and Conceptual Investigation', in Skaale, S. (Ed.), *The Right to National Self- Determination: The Faroe Islands and Greenland.* Boston: Martinus Nijhoff. 95–123.

Mitzen, J. 2006. 'Ontological Security in World Politics: State Identity and the Security Dilemma'. *European Journal of International Relations* 12(3): 341–370.

Rezvani, D.A. 2014. *Surpassing the Sovereign State: The wealth, Self-Rule, and Security*

Advantages of Partially Independent Territories. Oxford: Oxford University Press.

Seth, S. 2011, 'Postcolonial Theory and the Critique of International Relations', *Millennium,* Vol. 40 (1): 167–183

Sharman, J.C. 2013. 'International hierarchies and contemporary imperial governance: A tale of three kingdoms'. *European Journal of International Relations* 19(2): 189–207.

Sismondo S. 2017. Post-truth? *Social Studies of Science.*47(1): 3–6.

Steele, B. 2008. *Ontological Security in International Relations: Self-identity and the IR State.* Abingdon Routledge.

Stern, R., 2018. *The Gaslight Effect: How to Spot and Survive the Hidden Manipulation Others Use to Control Your Life*, 2nd ed. New York: Harmony Books.

Strandsbjerg, J. 2014. 'Making Sense of Contemporary Greenland: Indigeneity, Resources and Sovereignty', in: Powell, R. and Dodds, K. (Eds.), *Polar Geopolitics? Knowledges, Resources and Legal Regimes.* Cheltenham: Edward Elgar Publishing, pp. 259–276.

Subotic, J. and Zarakol, A. 2012. 'Cultural intimacy in International Relations'. *European Journal of International Relations* 19(4): 915–938.

Sweet, P. L. 2019. 'The Sociology of Gaslighting'. *American Sociological Review* 84(5):851– 875.

Turnowsky, W. 2019. 'Claus Hjort: Forholdet mellem Grønland og Danmark er blevet bedre' *Sermitsiaq* 01/02/2019. Available at: https://sermitsiaq.ag/ claus-hjortforholdet-mellem-groenland-danmark-blevet-bedre

Winkel Holm, K. 2020: 'Drop din forvanskning af Grønlands fortid, Aki-Maltida Høegh-Dam'. 22-07-2020. *Jyllands Posten.* Available at https://jyllands-posten.dk/debat/blogs/gamleblogs/katrineholm/ECE12298737/drop-din-forvanskning-af-groenlands-fortid-akimatilda-hoeeghdam/

Yu Untalan, C. 2020. Decentering the Self, Seeing Like the Other: Toward a Postcolonial Approach to Ontological Security, *International Political Sociology*, 14(1).

Zarakol, A. 2010 'Ontological (In)security and State Denial of Historical Crimes: Turkey and Japan'. *International Relations*.24(1): 3–23.

8

Digital Virulence and Post-Truth in Light of Baudrillard's Science-Fiction Theory of Pataphysics

SPIROS MAKRIS

> Digitality is with us.
> It is what which haunts all the messages,
> all the signs of our societies.
> – Baudrillard, 1983: 115

Jean Baudrillard's contribution to the discussion about the content and meaning of the postmodern condition remains important (Best and Kellner 1991, 111–145). His reflexive insights on the economic, ideological, cultural and technological phenomenon of neo-capitalism and so-called globalisation (Ritzer 2007), or whatever now is classified under the label of platform capitalism (Srnicek 2017), must be regarded as an integral component of a broader philosophical and theoretical discourse on the specific form and operation of post-war capitalism on a global scale (Ritzer 1997, 76–118). Specifically, from the 1970s onwards, more and more, a bunch of new and dynamic disciplines, approaches and methodologies, to name amongst others poststructuralism, postmodern theory, postcolonial studies, cultural studies, cyborg feminism and ecology, have raised the question of the catalytic role of technology in contemporary Western societies, drawing our attention to the advent of a posthuman condition (Best and Kellner 2001). In an innovative way, Baudrillard placed capitalist technology within the frame of digital virulence. Digitality is perceived as the 'turbine' of late capitalism, especially when it comes to the fields of information technology (IT), communication, mass media and social networks (Baudrillard 2012). It is not by chance that he speaks about a 'turbo-capitalism' (Makris 2018). The proliferation of digital technology has totally changed the epistemological, axiological, ideological, political and cultural characteristics of humanity. As in the similar cases of Haraway's cyborg feminism (Haraway 2004) and Braidotti's approach about a posthuman era (2013), Baudrillard brings to light the critical relation between man and machine or human and inhuman, stressing the process towards an anthropological shift in contemporary social ontology and phenomenology (Baudrillard 2000, 3–30).

IT, genetic cloning and Artificial Intelligence (AI) compose a basic analytical pillar in Baudrillard's social and political theory about late capitalism (Baudrillard 2008). If, as Haraway claims, the contemporary human being has been transformed into a cybernetic organism; or a hybrid of machine and organism; or a science-fiction creature (Haraway 2004, 7) – then, cybernetics, digital screens and genetic engineering play a crucial part in the transition of modern humanity to a posthuman age. By the same token, Braidotti asserts that this development in late modernity does not concern a post-naturalistic assumption of the modern world. Instead, it modifies the whole relationship between Nature and culture and chiefly the way that humanity places itself within a new existential condition (Braidotti 2013, 1–12). In all these pioneering approaches, information, communication and genetics affect largely the epistemological structure of social and political life in late capitalism, especially how we perceive the axiological and ethical justification of truth (Audi 2011). It is now clear that digital technology alters rapidly the epistemological limits of modern axiology and truth, bringing to focus the burning question of post-truth (Stenmark et al. 2018). The proliferation of information and communication via global media, platforms and networks undermine the cohesive view of modernity, revealing the multiple regimes of truth in a postmodern world that reign in relativism and post-truth. Through digital pluralism 'the real' is turned into a chaotic and liquid spectrality (Bauman 2000).

Digital technology and post-truth are critically connected to both the Covid-19 pandemic and climate change. On the one hand, we are witnesses to the ongoing process of a deconstruction of the human cell via genetics, medicine and technology, as happens with the vaccination engineering (Rezaei 2021). Technology creates a posthuman being, introducing at the same time world into so-called post-truth age: everything has been surrendered to the virulence of untrust, conspiracy theory and populism (Axford 2021). The rhetoric of Covid-19 has toxically merged with post-truth hate speech coming through the digital networks of platform capitalism (Lilleker et al. 2021). On the other hand, Covid-19 pushes humanity deeper in the bubble of digitisation. Despite the fact that the new approaches connect Covid-19 with the phenomena of the Anthropocene, climate change and a political theology of catastrophe (Delanty 2021) – social distancing as well as the digital tones of post-truth led late modernity to a situation of a onto-theological saturation. It is like, as Baudrillard claims, we have now exhausted all our potentialities. The global system has been entrapped into a condition of inertia, although everything seems to travel around the globe in record time.

Doubtless, Baudrillard has built the science-fiction theory of pataphysics as a holistic approach to the relations between technology, capitalism and globalisation, by paying attention to the extreme phenomena of simulation, simulacra and digitality. Postmodern condition pushes the human body, truth and nature to their limits (Baudrillard 1983). Given that, the chapter consists of five sections. The first section explores how postmodern axiological crisis tends to be turned into a digital and ecological dystopia. The second section analyses the relationship between mass media, masses and global politics. The third section examines Baudrillard's principle of reversibility with regard to reality and news. In the fourth section, cloning, AI and Baudrillard's concept of the 'Hell of the Same' are put within the problématique of true and false. The fifth and final section displays the provocative simulacrum of a zombie digital world.

From modern certainties to a post-truth digital and ecological dystopia?

Baudrillard connects the orders of simulacra and industrial technology with the questions of representation, appearance and counterfeit. In that respect, it could be claimed that simulation concerns a whole economic, political, ideological and cultural process in contemporary capitalist societies that turns false and fake into a new kind or reality, more real than the real: the hyperreal (Baudrillard 1983). So, knowledge, truth and artificiality are interconnected within the excessive technological reproducibility of capitalism (Benjamin 2008, 19–55). From this point of view, both simulacra and simulation can be seen as the critical steps towards a theory of post-truth – where reality collapses under the explosion of information, communication and news. Post-truth arises as social entropy in the age of digital technology, globalisation and populism (Nicholls 2016; Overell, Nicholls, 2020). Digital technology and political discourse prevail in the social ontology of post-truth in late modernity (Block 2019, 1). In most of cases, the relevant discussion is unfolding as a reflexive interrogation about disinformation, fake news and lying in politics (Dalkir and Katz 2020). Actually, this is not a new theoretical trend. In the 1970s, Hannah Arendt (1972, 1–47) drew our attention to the relationship between lies, truth and power. However, this remains a mainstream approach, so to speak. This chapter delivers a radical philosophical and theoretical perspective on the phenomenon of post-truth that is articulated with postmodern scepticism (Sim 2019) and Baudrillard's theory about simulacra and simulation (Kalpokas 2019, 103–104).

If we live in a postmodern condition, stigmatised by a new version of capitalism, i.e. 'platform', 'turbo' or 'tele-capitalism', Baudrillard (2011) builds a novel conceptual edifice that helps us to see things from a different point of view, revealing the catalytic role of IT, AI, genetics, mass media and digitality in contemporary social and political life (Baudrillard 1983). In fact, he has built a provocative science-fiction theory in which true and false are no longer considered as two separated situations, like good and evil in the conventional sense, but as the two faces of a new radical metaphysics: i.e. pataphysics (Baudrillard 1994, 1–9). In this new brave digital-driven postmodern and posthuman world, true and false are exchangeable either within a Manichean or a Nietzschean frame – where the reversibility principle and the pataphysical science-fiction theory of imaginary solutions dominate. Poetically speaking, he designates this onto-theological and anthropological metamorphosis of humanity in late capitalism as 'telemorphosis', pointing out that 'television has shown itself to be the strongest power within the science of imaginary solutions' (Baudrillard 2011, 29). Nothing anymore must be taken for granted. Everything attains its shape and meaning within a global network of digital circuits that has the pataphysical stamina to create entities without real referents. Living in a hyperreal world, in an ecstasy of communication (Baudrillard 2012, 19–30), or in a constant delirium of speed, as Paul Virilio (2006) claims from a similar viewpoint, in fact, we are travelling as object-signs through global digital platforms, desperately seeking for an Archimedean point. But, it is in vain.

For Baudrillard, since the 1980s, the postmodern world has entered into a dizzying orbital flight without a destination. Onto-theologically speaking, we live now in a condition emptied from meaning and reference. In Lefort's lexicon (1988, 19), everything is governed by the cataclysmic 'dissolution of the makers of certainty'. As information flows across the globe, through TV and digital screens, via demonic images (Baudrillard 2017, 13–31), true and false have become the blinking shades of a posthuman world that has been entirely sunk into the digital archipelago of indifference, contingency, obscenity and promiscuity. According to Baudrillard, this is not about good or bad. It is not a matter of ethics. Following in Nietzsche footsteps, he refers to an anthropological turn beyond good and evil, where the modern certainties no longer have any meaning or significance. In that respect, his analysis concerns a fatal condition that is dominated by extreme phenomena (Baudrillard 1993). Adopting Canetti's position about a deadly leap of modern humanity beyond reality and history, he claims that we are travelling in a void without even noticing it (Baudrillard 1990, 14).

Instead of a simple science-fiction theory of pataphysics, his systematic approach could be seen as an innovative New Critical Theory focusing on the crucial economic, technological, social, political, ideological and cultural changes that are taking place in late modernity (Makris, 2021). In order to constructively and imaginatively read these extreme changes of Western neo-capitalism on a global scale, we need a new and radical conceptual armoury. In a nutshell, we need a radical thought (Baudrillard 2008, 95–106). For him, the postmodern world, flooded by simulacra, screens, virtual realities, clones, information platforms and ecstatic communication, is a pornographic and virulent universe, in which the spectres of true and false are reversible (Baudrillard 2003, 25–30). It is interesting how, in the posthuman age of simulation and digitality, Paul Preciado (2019) applies Baudrillard's concepts of pornography and simulacra to human body, by placing artificial and modelled sexuality before anatomic reality itself.

Projecting our hyperreal existence through screens, circuits, platforms and networks, in fact, we occupy the perverse fortitude to make true and false according to the obscene needs of the moment. Baudrillard claims that the Cartesian ego lives now as a quasi-rational human being, lost in a chaotic and abyssal virtual space that he himself has diabolically overproduced. Putting an end to the modern binary realities of real and virtual, good and evil, true and false, etc., IT, AI, mass media, communication and simulation reinvent reality as a gigantic digital simulacrum amongst other extreme eventualities (Baudrillard 2006, 92–93). By doing so, post-humanity has almost been exhausted by her technological perversion. She looks like a contemporary Prometheus who has been transformed into a postmodern Frankenstein. The orgy of Western modernity has led the world into an artificial end of history (Baudrillard 1993, 3–13). The whole process seems like a vicious circle. To put it another way, it looks like a fatal strategy that brings to the fore a cool and ironic revenge coming from the side of the neglected objects themselves (Baudrillard 1990).

The excess of information and communication has turned into a condition of inertia – a bizarre immobility that appears like a frozen world. The posthuman world has already started the endless trek into the digital space of virtual redoubling, genetic cloning and AI (Baudrillard 2011a, 145–158). If we already live in a science-fiction future, without past and present, beyond reality and history, having exhausted all our human potentialities, then, it could be said that Baudrillard may reveal here the advent of a digital, as well as an ecological, dystopia. This is a critical situation we have to deal with, especially in light of new phenomena, such as Covid-19 and climate change, that exacerbate postmodern virulence.

Mass media, masses and the stupidity of politics in the age of globalisation

Trumpism, as an extreme transpolitical phenomenon, gives us the opportunity to move one step beyond the conventional wisdom of an allegedly moral and immoral power. For Baudrillard, this is pointless. Contemporary politics is not about honest politicians that speak the truth and vicious politicians that deceive the innocent people. This is a naïve approach that sees politics either as a romantic experience or as a way to manipulate crowds (Prado 2018). For him, global politics is nothing but a fatal strategy of a self-catastrophic stupidity. Contrary to mainstream Marxism and its alienation theory, Baudrillard (2007, 29–67) claims that in the age of globalisation the masses are accomplices to the perfect crime of politics. However, that is half the story. Actually, he claims that in late capitalism silent masses block hegemonic politics, through a process of involution that replaces the traditional problématique of revolution. Eventually, he comes to the conclusion that the masses have been nearly entrapped into the chaotic circuits of mass media and digital screens, leading the global system to ruins. This paradoxical and ironic situation, that saturating of the global system of power, destroys everything without an active rebellion, i.e. involution. For Baudrillard, in a postmodern world, we see the unfolding of two crucial procedures. First, politics and power are obsolete. In this vein, hegemon and masses are exchangeable simulacra via a fatal strategy of stupidity and involution. Second, hyperreality is rooted in global digital networks (Baudrillard 2007a).

Mass media constitutes the neuronal centre of hyperreality. As in Samuel Beckett's theatrical absurdism, we dwell in a brain that has been trapped in its simulacrum. Transcendence of God has been replaced by the immanence of genetic and digital codes (Baudrillard 1983, 109). We are imprisoned into the Platonic cave. Covid-19 could be regarded as another episode to this long industrial process of mediatisation and digitisation of human life (Delanty 2021, 107–121). Having lost every feeling of exteriority and otherness (Makris 2017; Makris 2021a), we cannot only find a way to make true and false or axiological judgments, but, in fact, we have lost every sense of reality and reference. Mass media, masses and digitality compose the dystopian scenery of global autism. Nevertheless, when Baudrillard talks about the demon of digital images, he does not mean a kind of a misfortune that reigns upon the world. On the contrary, he tries to reveal the Manichaean structure of postmodern condition. At the end of the day, so-called 'empire of good' is proven to be evil itself (Baudrillard 2010 and 2010a). The global system of power gives birth to international terrorism (Baudrillard 2012a). Who is good and who is bad? What is true and what is false? No longer is possible for us to distinguish moral from immoral. This is a transparent, superficial and flat world. Behind digital screens haunts an onto-theological void (Makris 2020).

Hyperreal relativism leads to an axiological crisis (Stenmark et al. 2018, 141–198). In the global age of transpolitics, transsexuality and transaesthetics, it is beyond our powers to judge good and bad, true and false or beautiful and ugly (Baudrillard 1993, 14–35). To the extent that postmodern world is flat, without transcendental depth – like a digital screen, packed with simulacra – this means that radical otherness has been eliminated in the fatal game of virtual copies. Ironically, the orgiastic passion for identity politics led to the tragic end of singularity. We dwell in a virtual void that seems like a huge digital pulp. Everything is distorted by the spectrality of digitality. As a huge black hole, simulacra absorb reality. The digital Minotaur devours humanity sending back a broadcasting version of hyperreality: i.e. artificial truths and lies of so-called 'real time'. Our daily lives are running out at the 8pm news. This is not merely about post-truth and the like; this is about digitality, hyperreality, posthuman condition and pataphysics (Baudrillard 1994, 2–9).

Baudrillard reads the extreme phenomena of simulacra in late modernity drawing his inspiration from Marshall McLuhan's axiom that medium dominates over the message (Baudrillard, 1996, 52). Message no longer expresses social ontology. Message is the medium itself (Baudrillard, 2019, 171–195). 'From medium to medium', he writes,

> the real is volatilized; it becomes an allegory of death, but it is reinforced by its very destruction; it becomes the real for the real, fetish of the lost object – no longer object of representation, but ecstasy of denegation and of its own ritual extermination: the hyperreal (Baudrillard 1983, 141–142).

Undoubtedly, this is a turning point in his analysis to the extent that although the ideological usage of digitality varies, bringing to light a heterogeneous multitude of individual and collective attitudes and behaviours, many of them are absolutely violent and racist. For example: online vitriol, lack of civility in the cybersphere, and anti-feminist rhetoric in social media (Jane 2014; Cole 2015). For Baudrillard, medium has the pervasive force to homogenise everything. In fact, digital simulacrum transforms messages into pure operations, without any real connection (Baudrillard 1983, 100). By digitising social, political and cultural activity, IT, AI, mass media, screens and communication networks evacuate human life from content. Digital instantaneity, i.e. 'real time', decodes and denervates any referent. Digitality distorts and controls meaning (Baudrillard 1983, 115–123).

Masses are absorbed into a hermetically closed global virtual circuit that reproduces them as a silent object sign. But, as mentioned above, this is half the story. While mass media inactivates masses – at the same time, the masses block mass media and global politics. It is worth pointing out here that the mediatised hyperreal world, composed of digital screens and simulacra, does not function as a mirror of truth and lies, but as a transparent and depthless void that devours every negativity and singularity (Baudrillard 1993, 111–174). Mass media is not a rational mechanism of verification and falsification. Instead, it works as an operational system that overproduces digital virulence in 'real time'. Having transformed masses into an enormous brain, without body and blood, mass media circulates in it the virtual viruses of pure simulacra on a 24/7 basis (Baudrillard 2000).

Despite the fact that Covid-19 brought to the fore the medical aspect of viruses, for Baudrillard, digital virulence stands in the very heart of late capitalism. It is no coincidence that he likens the ecstasy of communication to the situation of a cancerous metastasis. The excess of information destroys every possibility of meaning. The obscenity and promiscuity of mass media and digital screens nullifies every possibility to distinguish truth from falsehood. 'The contradictory process of true and false', he writes, 'of real and the imaginary, is abolished in this hyperreal logic' of mass media montage (Baudrillard 1983, 122). The exhaustion of reality murders the Real via the fatal strategy of perfect crime (Baudrillard 2008, 18). Nonetheless, it is important to remember that digitality means complicity. The masses participate in a post-orgy condition in which lies, fake news and trolling are not but the obese expression of a pornographic world (Happer et al. 2019). Digitality turns capitalism into a gigantic stage, where humanity exists performing in 'real time'. As in a reality show, masses can only live through screen and simulacra. However, this is in vain. Digital hyperreality evacuates any message, distorts truth and false and corrupts axiological judgment. Only mass media, networks and platforms can deliver the pretext of objectivity.

In the postmodern and posthuman world, true and false are empty signifiers that are floating in the depthless space of global digitality. As pixels, they unstoppably change in a dizzying void full of bizarre simulacra. Paraphrasing Heraclitus, it could be said that everything is given birth through a digital war (Merrin 2019). Following in Baudrillard's footsteps, Merrin (2005) asserts that the digital screen 'is killing the art of symbolic exchange'. In other words, the electronic demon of simulacra turns human life into a delirious spectacle of non-events.

Reversibility principle, reality, and the political economy of TV fantasies

Globalisation, where a political economy of virtual news reigns, could be seen as a Manichaean digital war of principles. This is a key aspect in Baudrillard's pataphysics that brings to the fore the principle of reversibility. The postmodern world is not a monistic universe. Instead, it looks like a pendulum that swings unstoppably between reversible positions. So, acceleration is turned into inertia. Good is turned into evil. Truth and falsehood are interchanging situations. Reversibility is the metonymy of excess. Henceforth, we dwell in a world that works in a state of existential and phenomenological exaggeration. It is an obscene world full of extreme phenomena (Baudrillard

1990, 25–70). The delirium of mass media digitality takes the form of an immanent deification in the fascinating and seductive ritual of evening news: i.e. TV fantasies (Baudrillard 2002, 186–190). However, it is not simply about virtuality. Digitality, as an accelerated spectrum of media news as a whole, operates into the void. TV, video, screens, multimedia, the internet, platforms and networks have cancelled any possibility of moral judgment (Baudrillard 2002, 176). Even the global system cannot control the exponential proliferation of information. Social media pushes it to its onto-theological limits: i.e. the agony of power (Baudrillard 2010a). True and false are being merged into a semantic confusion. Who has the fortitude to verify the validity of news, while they are running across the globe, through endless circuits, building an enormous pile of digital rubbish? Albert Camus says that humanity must pay the heavy price of her metaphysical rebellion (Camus 2000, 29). Modern Prometheus has been enslaved to the demonic space of virtual images and digital news. Reality has been replaced by the hyperrealism of simulation and simulacra. The hyperreal, Baudrillard asserts, means that the 'contradiction between the real and the imaginary is effaced. The unreal is no longer that of dream or of fantasy, of a beyond or a within, it is that of a hallucinatory resemblance of the real with itself' (Baudrillard 1983, 142).

As we have seen, Baudrillard (1990, 111–179) rejects the Marxist theory of alienation. In this brave new mediatised world, simulacra, TV fantasies and digitality compose a pataphysical order of objectivity. He repeatedly refers to a kind of objective irony that leads humanity to a situation of cool revenge. Object-signs reign upon human subjects. In that sense, the reversibility principle and turbo-capitalism reveal a postmodern Apocalypse. His provocative science-fiction theory may shed light on a digital dystopia that more and more turns into an ecological dystopia. As pointed out earlier, both Covid-19 and climate change could be regarded as new episodes towards this risky process of global virulence. On his paradoxical account, salvation is translated into a kind of self-catastrophe. It looks like an ancient Greek drama. Hubris via nemesis leads to catharsis. He places this chain of events on the basis of a radical onto-theological destiny. As a contemporary Luther, he approaches redemption of world through its ruin. Following Walter Benjamin's messianic political theology, he crafts a postmodern *Angelus Novus* that leads humanity to heaven through hell. Provocatively speaking, he terms this pataphysical process the intelligence of evil (Baudrillard, 2005).

Baudrillard builds a theory of simulacra in which the object-sign of mass media news prevails. Since the 1960s he has drawn our attention to the catalytic role of information, communication and images in late capitalism. He places technological developments, and especially digitality, at the epicentre of postmodernity. Neo-capitalist reality brings to the fore hyperreality. By doing so, he displays the end of metaphysics and the advent of pataphysics.

Sometimes, he speaks as a postmodern physicist. In fact, through physics, he transforms metaphysics into a science-fiction theory. To put it another way, he uses physics and developments in IT, AI, communication and genetics in order to unveil the onto-theological limits of posthuman condition (Baudrillard 2000, 1–30). Hyperreality concerns the replacement of real life from 'real time', through a political economy of viral news and images. More specifically, digital technology transforms late capitalism into a laboratory of global simulacra. At the end of the day, the dizzying, speedy and chaotic character of digital technology leads to a new cosmogenesis. Having absorbed by the abyssal TV fantasies, mass media and digital screens, humanity loses not only her tangible body, but her brain, that is to say her rationalistic capability to translate social ontology and phenomenology into a stable, sensible and comprehensive axiological system of true and false connotations (Baudrillard 2008, 21–25).

From this perspective, the political economy of simulacra and simulation puts the postmodern world in peril. The lack of transcendental depth, even the depth of the human mind itself, leaves humanity without a steady system of cognitive and ethical reckoning. The new measure of things is a digital image that travels across the globe via screens, circuits, platforms and networks. Nihilism is no longer about a dead God or the so-called end of history. Posthuman nihilism concerns the implosion of meaning in the mass media; the implosion of the social in the silent masses; the parodic, ironic and fatal strategy of a more and more accelerated inertia (Baudrillard 1994a, 161). In Heideggerian terms, it seems like *Dasein* has dived into onto-theological oblivion. Trapped and lost in the Khôra of a digital coma, the world travels without moral guidance, meaning and essence. Being flat, meaningless and chaotic, postmodern humanity has been subjugated to the pataphysical destiny of an objective and cool irony. Poetically speaking, it could be claimed that a grotesque laughter is raised now above world, distorting every trace of human physicality. In Marx's parlance, it could be said that a spectre haunts world: the spectre of digitality.

Cloning, AI and the apotheosis of the 'Hell of the Same'

In a postmodern world that seems like an enormous media laboratory, Baudrillard (2000, 3–30) shifts his analysis to cloning in the sense of a generic category of phenomena, not only genetic but chiefly digital. For some social scientists, we have already entered into the global age of digital cloning, flooded by tones of human digital thought clones (Truby and Brown, 2021). For some other social analysts, this is the age of digital immortality and virtual humanity (Savin-Baden and Burden, 2019). In that respect, AI could be perceived as a gigantic digital brain that pointlessly stores every aspect of posthuman life (Baudrillard 2011a, 158).

Cloning and AI compose the essential processes of digitality in late capitalism. Both demonstrate the apotheosis of sameness, so to speak. In fact, the homogenisation of negativity and singularity via simulation and simulacra, with the exponential proliferation of social media communication, TV fantasies and IT, leads postmodern world to the 'Hell of the Same' (Baudrillard 1993, 113–123). Using so-called smart electronic devices all around the clock, we have been transformed into homogenised clones and replicas of virtual simulacra. In onto-theological terms, it is like we have achieved the Promethean feat to recreate cybernetic, cyborg and posthuman ourselves as an omnipresent and omnipotent digital god (Harari 2017). Digital cloning brings to the fore the axiological and ethical anxieties of social cloning, cloning cultures and socio-cultural sameness (Essed and Goldberg 2002). Cloning and AI pave the way for a homogenized world mindset. Everybody is technologically and virulently pushed to think and express themselves the same way, using the same digital software. Baudrillard speaks about a global 'massage' of human thinking, acting and judging (Baudrillard 1983, 124).

It is no longer about true and false, good and bad or beautiful and ugly. Modern cognitive, ethical and aesthetical pluralism is obsolete. Who cares about true and false when everyone immerses themselves into the digital habitat of sameness? Every single moment of the day, we offer ourselves as prey to this postmodern Minotaur: i.e. digital homogenisation. No more faces, only digital simulacra. No more events, only digital news. No more rationality, only AI. No more singularity, only the dread of sameness. Entering the age of digital posthumanity, flooded by electronic devices and virtual images, in fact, we have been entrapped into a digital enchantment, leaving behind every trace of human frail and reality (Bishop 2011, 349). Henceforth, human physicality seems like an abnormal exemption. The dominant trend is to live like a digital replica and think like a digital clone. This is the hyperreality of posthumanity. Transhumanists herald the advent of a digital religion. Digital sameness preaches a digital wellbeing, where every virtual human tends to look the same, behave the same and features the same digital operationalities. It is no coincidence that more and more the idea of a post-truth age is intertwined with mass media, IT, AI, cloning and digitality (Gibaroğlu 2019; Lacković 2020).

If in the final analysis the digital era is realised as a post-truth age – some invoke a sort of media literacy to distinguish truth from lies, to deconstruct information and communication disorder, and to achieve an axiological and ethical accuracy (Friesem 2019). In this vein, a post-truth condition in the digital era could be considered as an onto-theological and an epistemological crisis (Angermuller 2018). As posthumanity proceeds towards a new, radical and extreme technological context, i.e. the digital order of simulacra, it is difficult to keep her conventional metaphysical status. If we have passed the critical point of human horizon, as Canetti claims, travelling beyond historical time, we need a new metaphysical guidance. Given that, it can be claimed that Baudrillard builds the imaginative toolkit of pataphysics to help us cope with the postmodern complexities of hyperreality (Baudrillard 2003).

Living as virtual zombies in a screen universe? A provocative prognosis

In Nietzschean terms, it is no longer about good and evil. In posthuman era, everything is about sameness and complicity. Virtual masses fervently take part in a fatal game of homogenisation. The global system of mass media and social networks – that is to say either 'platform' or 'turbo' or 'tele-capitalism' – does not concern the situation of servitude, but the condition of complicity. Contrary to the Marxist narrative of alienation, post-humanity is accomplice to the digitisation of everything. Everybody wants to play this fascinating game of digital cloning and virtual human. Talking about a perfect crime, Baudrillard (2008) means a bizarre condition, in which there is no crime, predators, victims and motivations. If the digital world is a neutral world, then no human singularity exists. Medically speaking, we are approaching the condition of a hyperreal media-driven death. Posthuman cardiogram seems like a straight line, but, in a paradoxical and ironic sense, we continue to live like zombies do. Don DeLillo and Neil Postman's media dystopias are now fully alive (DeLillo 1999; Postman 2006).

Is this science-fiction prognosis of a digital-led human destiny true or false? Could it be the actual question of the so-called post-truth age? Is it feasible for contemporary humanity to cross over the historical horizon, by transforming herself into a postmodern digital replica? Is digitality, as Baudrillard constantly says (1996, 66), our new normality? Telling personal stories, or providing resistance against racism and sexism (Barlow and Awan 2016) in a dynamic virtual context, is regarded as a positive aspect of this massive digitality that overflows capitalism in the age of globalisation, post-truth, viruses and climate change (Dayter and Mühleisen 2016). On the other hand, there is an analytical tendency that sees the apocalyptic advent of a digital zombie world in these extreme technological and cultural developments. The provocative discourse about zombie media and 'digital dead' occupies a foundational position within the current debate about digitality, hyperreality and post-humanity (Schott 2010; Cameron 2012; Olofsson 2013; Iannella 2017).

References

Angermuller, Johannes. (2018). 'Truth after post-truth: for a Strong Programme in Discourse Studies', *Palgrave Communications*, 4(30): 1–8.

Arendt, Hannah. (1972). *Crises of the Republic*. New York: Harcourt Brace Jovanovich, Inc.

Audi, Robert. (2011). *Epistemology. A Contemporary Introduction to the Theory of Knowledge. Third Edition*. London and New York: Routledge.

Axford, Barrie. (2021). *Populism vs the New Globalization*. London: Sage.

Barlow, Charlotte and Awan, Imran. (2016). '"You Need to Be Sorted Out With a Knife": The Attempted Online Silencing of Women and People of Muslim Faith Within Academia', *Social Media + Society*, October-December: 1–11.

Baudrillard, Jean. (1983). *Simulations*. New York: Semiotext(e) (Translated by Paul Foss, Paul Patton and Philip Beitchman).

Baudrillard, Jean. (1990). *Fatal Strategies*. New York: Semiotext(e) (Translated by Philip Beitchman and W. G. J. Niesluchowski).

Baudrillard, Jean. (1993). *The Transparency of Evil. Essays on Extreme Phenomena*. London, New York: Verso (Translated by James Benedict).

Baudrillard, Jean. (1994). *The Illusion of the End*. Cambridge: Polity Press (Translated by Chris Turner).

Baudrillard, Jean. (1994a). *Simulacra and Simulation*. Ann Arbor: The University of Michigan Press (Translated by Sheila Faria Glaser).

Baudrillard, Jean. (1996). *Cool Memories II 1987–1990*. Durham, NC: Duke University Press (Translated by Chris Turner).

Baudrillard, Jean. (2000). *The Vital Illusion*. New York: Columbia University Press (Edited by Julia Witwer).

Baudrillard, Jean. (2002). *Screened Out*. London, New York: Verso (Translated by Chris Turner).

Baudrillard, Jean. (2003). *Passwords*. London, New York: Verso (Translated by Chris Turner).

Baudrillard, Jean. (2005). *The Intelligence of Evil or the Lucidity Pact*. Oxford: Berg (Translated by Chris Turner).

Baudrillard, Jean. (2006). *Cool Memories V 2000-2004*. Cambridge: Polity Press (Translated by Chris Turner).

Baudrillard, Jean. (2007). *Forget Foucault*. Los Angeles, CA: Semiotext(e) (Translated by Phil Beitchman, Lee Hildreth, and Mark Polizzotti).

Baudrillard, Jean. (2007a). *In the Shadow of the Silent Majorities*. Los Angeles, CA: Semiotext(e) (Translated by Paul Foss, John Johnston, Paul Patton, and Andrew Berardini).

Baudrillard, Jean. (2008). *The Perfect Crime*. London, New York: Verso (Translated by Chris Turner).

Baudrillard, Jean. (2010). *Carnival and Cannibal*. London, New York, Calcutta: Seagull Books (Translated by Chris Turner).

Baudrillard, Jean. (2010a). *The Agony of Power*. Los Angeles, CA: Semiotext(e) (Translated by Ames Hodges).

Baudrillard, Jean. (2011). *Telemorphosis*. Minneapolis, MN: Univocal (Translated by Drew S. Burk).

Baudrillard, Jean. (2011a). *Impossible Exchange*. London, New York: Verso (Translated by Chris Turner).

Baudrillard, Jean. (2012). *The Ecstasy of Communication*. South Pasadena, CA: Semiotext(e) (Translated by Bernard Schütze and Caroline Schütze).

Baudrillard, Jean. (2012a). *The Spirit of Terrorism*. London, New York: Verso (Translated by Chris Turner).

Baudrillard, Jean. (2017). *The Evil Demon Of Images*. Waterloo: The Power Institute of Fine Arts (Translated by Paul Patton and Paul Foss).

Baudrillard, Jean. (2019). *For a Critique of the Political Economy of the Sign*. London, New York: Verso (Translated by Charles Levin).

Bauman, Zygmunt. (2000). *Liquid Modernity*. Cambridge: Polity Press.

Benjamin, Walter. (2008). *The Work of Art in the Age of Its Technological Reproducibility, and Other Writings on Media*. Cambridge, Massachusetts: Harvard University Press (Translated by Edmund Jephcott, Rodney Livingstone, Howard Eiland, and Others).

Best, Steven and Kellner, Douglas. (1991). *Postmodern Theory. Critical Interrogations*. London: Macmillan.

Best, Steven and Kellner, Douglas. (2001). *The Postmodern Adventure. Science, Technology, and Cultural Studies at the Third Millennium*. New York, London: The Guildford Press.

Bishop, Rebecca. (2011), 'The Dread of Sameness', *Cultural Studies Review*, 7(1): 349–354.

Block, David. (2019). *Post-Truth and Political Discourse*. Switzerland: Palgrave Macmillan.

Braidotti, Rosi. (2013). *The Posthuman*. Cambridge: Polity Press.

Cameron, Allan. (2012). 'Zombie Media. Transmission, Reproduction, and the Digital Dead', *Cinema Journal*, 52(1): 66–89.

Camus, Albert. (2000). *The Rebel*. London: Penguin Books (Translated by Anthony Bower).

Cole, Kirsti K. (2015). '"It's Like She's Eager to Be Verbally Abused": Twitter, Trolls, and (En)gendering Disciplinary Rhetoric', Feminist Media Studies, 15(2): 356–358.

Dalkir, Kimiz, Katz, Rebecca, eds. (2020). *Navigating Fake News, Alternative Facts, and Misinformation in a Post-Truth World*. Hershey, PA, USA: IGI Global.

Dayter, Daria and Mühleisen, Susanne. (2016). 'Telling Stories about Self in Digital Contexts: Same, Same, but Different?', *Open Linguistics*, 2: 572–576.

Delanty, Gerard, ed. (2021). *Pandemics, Politics, and Society. Critical Perspectives on the Covid-19 Crisis*. Berlin, Boston: De Gruyter.

DeLillo, Don. (1999). *White Noise*. New York: Penguin Books.

Essed, Philomena and Goldberg, David Theo. (2002). 'Cloning cultures: the social injustices of sameness', *Ethic and Radical Studies*, 25(6): 1066–1082.

Friesem, Yonty. (2019). 'Teaching Truth, Lies, and Accuracy in the Digital Age: Media Literacy as Project-Based Learning', *Journalism & Mass Communication Educator*, 74(2): 185-198.

Gibaroğlu, Mehmet Oytun. (2019). 'Post-Truth in Social Media', *The Archival World*, 6(2): 87–99.

Happer, Catherine, Hoskins, Andrew, Merrin, William, eds. (2019). *Trump's Media War*. Switzerland: Palgrave Macmillan.

Harari, Yuval Noah. (2017). *Homo Deus. A Brief History of Tomorrow*. New York: Harper.

Haraway, Donna. (2004). *The Haraway Reader*. New York and London: Routledge.

Iannella, Renato. (2017). 'Tragedy of the Digital Commons: Amplified Zombies', *IEEE Technology and Society Magazine*, September: 15–16.

Jane, Emma A. (2014). '"Your a Ugly, Whorish, Slut". Understanding E-bile', *Feminist Media Studies*, 14(4): 531–546.

Kalpokas, Ignas. (2019). *A Political Theory of Post-Truth*. Switzerland: Palgrave Macmillan.

Lacković, Nataša. (2020). 'Thinking with Digital Images in the Post-truth age: A Method in Critical Media Literacy', *Postdigital Science and Education*, 2: 442–462.

Lefort, Claude. (1988). *Democracy and Political Theory*. Cambridge: Polity Press (Translated by David Macey).

Lilleker, Darren et al., eds. (2021). *Political Communication and Covid-19. Governance and Rhetoric in Times of Crisis*. London and New York: Routledge.

Makris, Spiros. (2017). 'Politics, Ethics and Strangers in the 21st Century. Fifteen critical reflections on Jacques Derrida's concept of hos(ti)pitality', *Theoria & Praxis. International Journal of Interdisciplinary Thought*, 5(1): 1–21.

Makris, Spiros. (2018). 'Masses, Turbo-capitalism and Power in Jean Baudrillard's Social and Political Onto-theology', *International Journal of Theology, Philosophy and Science*, 2(3): 91–112.

Makris, Spiros. (2020). 'The concept of terror in Jean Baudrillard's social ontology', *Dia-noesis. A Journal of Philosophy*, 8: 49–65.

Makris, Spiros. (2021). 'European IPT as a new critical theory of world politics. The instructive case of Jean Baudrillard', in *Perspectives on International Political Theory in Europe*, edited by Vassilios Paipais, 129-146. New York: Palgrave Macmillan.

Makris, Spiros. (2021a). 'Politics of space, strangeness, and culture in the global age', in *Political Sociologies of the Cultural Encounter. Essays on Borders, Cosmopolitanism and Globalization*, edited by Barrie Axford, Alistair Brisbourne, Sandra Halperin, and Claudia Lueders, 39–53. London and New York: Routledge.

Merrin, William. (2005). *Baudrillard and the Media. A Critical Introduction*. Cambridge: Polity Press.

Merrin, William. (2019). *Digital War. A Critical Introduction*. Cambridge: Polity Press.

Nicholls, Brett. (2016). 'Baudrillard in a "Post-Truth" World: Groundwork for a Critique of the Rise of Trump', *MEDIANZ*, 16(2): 7–30.

Olofsson, Jennie. (2013). '"Zombies Ahead!" A study of how hacked digital road signs destabilize the physical space of roadways', *Visual Communication*, 13(1): 75–93.

Overell, Rosemary, Nicholls, Brett, eds. (2020). *Post-Truth and the Mediation of Reality. New Conjunctures*. Switzerland: Palgrave Macmillan.

Postman, Neil. (2016). *Amusing Ourselves to Death. Public Discourse in the Age of Show Business*. New York: Penguin Book.

Prado, C. G. (2018). *America's Post-Truth Phenomenon. When Feelings and Opinions Trump Facts and Evidence*. Santa Barbara, California: Praeger.

Preciado, Paul. (2019). *Pornotopia. An Essay on Playboy's Architecture and Biopolitics*. New York: Zone Books.

Rezaei, Nima, ed. (2021). *Coronavirus Disease – Covid-19*. Switzerland: Springer.

Ritzer, George. (1997). *Postmodern Social Theory*. New York: The McGraw-Hill Companies, Inc.

Ritzer, George, ed. (2007). *The Blackwell Companion to Globalization*. Oxford: Blackwell Publishing.

Savin-Baden, Maggi and Burden, David. (2019). 'Digital Immortality and Virtual Humans', *Postdigital Science and Education*, 1: 87–103.

Schott, Gareth. (2010). 'Dawn of the Digital Dead: The Zombie as Interactive Social Satire in American Popular Culture', *Australasian Journal of American Studies*, 29(1): 69–75.

Sim, Stuart. (2019). *Post-Truth, Scepticism & Power*. Switzerland: Palgrave Macmillan.

Srnicek, Nick. (2017). *Platform Capitalism*. Cambridge: Polity Press.

Stenmark, Mikael, Fuller, Steve, Zackariasson, Ulf, eds. (2018). *Relativism and Post-Truth in Contemporary Society. Possibilities and Challenges*. Switzerland: Palgrave Macmillan.

Truby, Jon and Brown, Rafael. (2021). 'Human digital thought clones: the *Holy Grail* of artificial intelligence for big data', *Information & Communications Technology Law*, 30(2): 140–168.

Virilio, Paul. (2006). *Speed and Politics*. Los Angeles, CA: Semiotext(e) (Translated by Mark Polizzotti).

9

The Challenges of Epistemic Communities in Shaping Policy in the Age of Post-Truth

ATAL AHMADZAI

The scope and implications of global threats often transcend nation-states' jurisdictional and territorial boundaries. By creating inevitable trans-planetary connectivity and interdependencies, globalization and its associated threats have challenged the effectiveness of state-centered interventions and, for that reason, have instigated the need for global governance. In the absence of an overarching authority, global governance aims to manage interdependencies caused by transnational threats and issues (Rosenau 1999). Accordingly, different approaches have been expounded to govern and manage these threats, including policy networks, epistemic communities, interest groups, advocacy groups, issue networks, and international organisations. These approaches focus on the involvement, nature, and authority of the actors involved in the global policy enterprise (Sending 2015). In other words, actors within these approaches compete for authority. For that reason, each approach claims a different source of legitimacy, including institutional, expert, moral, or delegated.

The emergence of post-truth politics has deepened global governance's authority and legitimacy challenges at the policy making and implementation levels. Sensationalised, provoked, and emotionally driven public opinions on issues such as climate change, public health, immigration, and others push global policy initiatives toward fragmentation and disintegration. Populism, driven mainly by simplistic explanations, the fast and furious spread of misinformation, and the conspiratorial understanding of given issues (Bergmann 2020, 251-65), has erected new obstacles for policy on issues with global scope and implications. The authority and legitimacy of transnational actors is challenged or rejected by the polarised and mostly nationalised public opinion of post-truth politics. Such limitations are more consequential in political and social contexts where democratic deliberations are essential for policymaking.

Returning to science and facts has been promoted as the antithesis of the post-truth age and socialisation. Science as a fact-based enterprise should be an accepted central source of authority for informed reflection. One approach with claim to science and facts is the notion of epistemic communities – 'networks of professionals with recognised expertise and competence in a particular domain, who withhold an authoritative claim to policy-relevant knowledge within that domain or issue-area' (Haas 1992, 03). Unlike interest-based or normative approaches, the significance of epistemic communities is their empirical and objective orientation. As a knowledge-policy nexus, the approach should be consequential for global policy outcomes in the age of post-truth politics. The question, however, arises concerning the practicality of this approach in the realm of democratic politics in the post-truth age, where polarised discourses, beliefs, ideologies, and emotions are more influential in shaping public opinion. Furthermore, with the democratisation of knowledge creation and dissemination due to technological advances and social media, the post-truth age challenges epistemic communities' authoritative claim to knowledge and facts and their interpretations for policy consumption. Therefore, it can be argued that in an age characterised by the rejection of monopolising information, facts, and knowledge, epistemic communities do not serve as a solution but as part of the problem. An elitist approach to issues and policies can further stir populist controversies and strengthen the rejection of authority over the production, interpretation, and dissemination of facts, if not facts per se.

This chapter is built around three sections. The first section looks at the evolution of the concept of epistemic communities. It discusses how a promising concept in a time characterised by hyperglobalism (the early 1990s) could not stand its ground as an approach to global governance. The second section deconstructs post-truth politics. By destabilising the link between objectivity and Enlightenment, the section argues that untruths, distorted facts, and misinformation have been prevalent in public discourses and politics since the European Enlightenment. The current hype about the post-truth politics is due to the losing grip of elite circles in Western societies over the monopoly of constructing and disseminating master narratives and discourses for channelling distorted facts, misinformation, and untruths. The third section explores the theoretical and practical challenges associated with epistemic communities' approach to dealing with global governance in the age of 'post-truth.'

Epistemic communities: An approach for global governance

Realism, and later neoliberalism, have dominated International Relations (IR) theory for most of its evolutionary age. Despite conceptualising the nature and dynamics of the international system differently, these approaches converge on the unmalleability and fixed nature of state interests, which constrain state's behaviour on the international stage. However, these mainstream and positivist IR paradigms could not adequately explain states' uncertainty regarding their respective interests in the age of globalisation. The emergence of transnational threats and structural issues has caused uncertainty and misperceptions about states' interests, which are the underlying reasons for conflicts in international relations (Stein 1990, 55). Uncertainty and misperceptions about states' interests have inspired and shaped new patterns in states' behaviour for realising new interests in a rapidly transforming and unpredictable international milieu. Accordingly, such dynamics expanded the scope of intellectual inquiries in International Relations to the new frontiers of global governance. New analytical approaches and tools for explaining and comprehending the socialisation of states on a globalising international stage have emerged. Research on epistemic communities is one of many bodies of literature that seeks to explain patterns of states' behaviour in an uncertain and complex global context.

As a conceptual framework within the constructivist IR paradigm, the epistemic communities approach explores the coordination of global governance in an interconnected and interdependent world (Haas 1992, 1–35). It explains the authority, role, and effects of experts in global affairs. Haas identified four defining characteristics for epistemic communities: shared normative and causal beliefs, shared notions of validity, and common policy enterprise. Unlike interest-based and normative approaches to global policy – such as policy networks, interest groups, and issue networks that are engaged in political exchanges to secure better stakes – epistemic communities scrutinise issues exclusively under a scientific lens. It is considered more instrumental to effective policy formulation and tangible outcomes. As an example, the approach was deemed influential in shaping some directives and consensus of the European Union (Haas 2016, 08). However, it could not seem to evolve beyond its initial conceptualisation and became marginalised (Cross 2013, 137). Different aspects of the concept have been scrutinised to understand the reasons behind its stagnation, including the political autonomy and orientation of experts, the vague definition of experts, confusion about the target audience (state only or non-state actors as well), the application of science-based arguments in public policy and discourses, and the lack of an analytical tool to explain the consensus on the authoritative claim to knowledge.

While the proponents of epistemic communities have responded to such criticism, a novel area of inquiry about these communities is their application and implications in the post-truth age. Thus, while the concept has emerged to coordinate and facilitate informed policy initiatives in a globalising world with prevailing uncertainties, contemporary post-truth politics have introduced the concept to new challenges. Before exploring these, it is essential to shed light on the emerging narrative of the post-truth age.

International Relations (IR) in the age of post-truth politics

Post-truth is a relatively new adjective in the domestic and global political lexicon. In the age of globalisation, the implications of post-truth politics are directed at societies' collective intellectual reflection on issues with national and transnational scope. As such, post-truth politics have effects on international politics and global governance, mainly in societies with democratic deliberations on policy making. It can be inferred that rather than being informed by the objective reflection of the truth of reality, the circumstances related to the post-truth drive the orientation of public and global policy initiatives towards populistic socialisation.

The unexpected rise in narratives related to post-truth politics resulted in widely varying accounts of what caused it to emerge. However, many existing explanations fail to revel the substantive aspects of the problem. The RAND Corporation, for example, identified the transformation and proliferation of conventional and social media, the spread of disinformation, and polarisation as drivers of 'truth decay' (Kavanagh and Rich 2018, 79). Such is a simplistic description of a complex and multidimensional issue. While the proliferation of information sources can facilitate a conducive environment for disseminating both facts or lies, restricting or monopolising these sources have social, political, and moral implications. Furthermore, having control over sources of information does not mean the objectivity of information or the reality of truth. It only restricts the plurality of given narratives in favour of the status quo.

Lewandowsky et al. (2017, 356) relate the 'malaise' of post-truth to the creation of alternative epistemic spaces as platforms for sharing alternative realities. Similarly, Fuller (2016) argues that the post-truth age results from the universalisation of symmetry or epistemic democratisation. Such perspectives hold post-truth as circumstances facilitated by the proliferation of information production and dissemination instruments. Once again, these accounts exclusively focus on the tools and platforms (conventional vs. popular, or mainstream vs. alternative) of information, not on the underlying processes and structures involved in producing information and knowledge. Accordingly, in an editorial, the *Social Studies of Science* (2017, 3) argues that while the production of scientific knowledge requires infrastructure, effort, ingenuity, and validation structures, the current popular information tools destroy these structures. In general, existing explanations of the post-truth age revolve around the role of social media and other alternative information platforms. They point to the diminishing role of scientific knowledge, objectivity, and facts in shaping public opinion, politics, and policy initiatives. Such comprehensions seem to be based on the assumed role of conventional sources and spaces of information in socialising public opinion with objectivity. The question, however, is if conventional sources truly disseminate facts and objective information?

Scrutinising against the theoretical and practical aspects of objectivity and facts in informing public opinion, the rigor and robustness of existing comprehensions about post-truth politics are questionable. Notably, in the milieu of International Relations, conceptual and practical relationships between objectivity and facts with politics and public opinion are complex. Therefore, it is essential to have a theoretical discussion on the subjectivity of truth and a brief retrospective look at the Western powers' long tradition of politicising realities and distorting facts to shape public opinion. These two discussions reveal a complicated picture of truth and objectivity in the political sphere.

Science and 'Truth'

Truth is a philosophical concept, and plenty of controversies are associated with the simple statement of 'what is truth?' (Glanzberg, 2021). It has a strong subjective appeal and is shaped by personal convictions and opinions. Therefore, truth is contested. As a belief-based enterprise, the popularity or universality of a 'truth' does not make it factual or objective, per se. These characteristics complicate the relationship of truth with science, for that reason, with facts. Within the realm of scientific knowledge, the purpose of inquiry is not about truth. Scientific inquiry and its different epistemologies confront or support a position, idea, thesis, and theory with facts and evidence. This is to draw a clear line between scientific and non-scientific endeavours, such as authoritative knowledge. While the beliefs and personal convictions of an overwhelming number of people can constitute a 'truth' this does not necessarily constitute 'facts', as these 'truths' can be based in superstition or other unprovable mental processes, such as beliefs.

Furthermore, as a self-restraint measure and to avoid transforming to a belief-based enterprise that is not only unquestionable but at the same time equally unprovable, scientific inquiry applies anticipatory processes. These make science open to challenge and change. Within the complex field of philosophy and history of scientific knowledge, explanations such as the 20th century's probabilism, Karl Popper's falsifiability (Popper 2002), Thomas Kuhn's paradigm shift (Kuhn 2012), and Lakatos's research program (Lakatos 1980) identified different mechanisms and structures for the internal consistency of and progress in scientific knowledge. Consequently, while not directly dealing with truth, scientific knowledge actively evolves to defy becoming a belief-based enterprise that can neither be disproved nor subject to argument and challenge.

These arguments do not imply to justify the manifestations of the post-truth politics, such as deceptions, lies, and misinformation in the public sphere. However, the point is that the concept of truth is a complicated philosophical construct that can hardly be squared within the fundamental characteristics of scientific inquiry, including falsifiability, testability, generalisability, and parsimony. Truth is a multifaceted, delicate, and loaded notion that even those who talk about post-truth avoid talking about the 'truth'. For example, RAND Corporation, in its report on 'Truth Decay', while using the phrase 'truth decay' hundreds of times, the term 'truth' however, is used not more than a handful of times and that exclusively in the context of disclaiming discussing the truth (see Kavanagh and Rich 2018). Similarly, Kakutani (2018), unlike what the book's topic reads – *The Death of Truth* – did not discuss truth but focused on 'the fall of reasons' or 'the vanishing of reality'. Even though these three – truth, reality, and reasons – are separate and different elements of mental processes.

The intellectual context surrounding the philosophical juggernaut about discussing 'truth' is understandable. Truth has a pervasive use in ordinary language. However, its meaning, interpretation, and comprehension are nothing but intellectually nebulous. As such, where does this leave the conceptualisation of the term post-truth? A logical fallacy. While the premise 'truth' cannot be straightforwardly conceptualised, at least intellectually, the conclusion – 'post-truth' – also is challenging to hold up to scrutiny. Nevertheless, it does not mean that prevailing manifestations of the construct of post-truth – such as lies, dis/misinformation, and deceptions – should be acceptable. However, it also must be acknowledged that the contemporary manifestations of post-truth politics are not novel in the domestic and international domains. In retrospect, the history of modern politics, mainly in a democratic setting, is hardly based on communicating pure facts and evidence. In international relations, the manifestations of post-truth politics has been there forever. This leads us to briefly look at the history of Western powers' use of distorted facts, lies, and deceptions in public discourses for shaping public opinion.

The politicised utilisation of facts

Misinformation, fake news, lies, deceptions, and erosion of trust in facts and reality are identified as the manifestations of post-truth politics (Lewandowsky et al. 2017, 364). These ills are even considered deliberate efforts against the broader idea of sanity (Gopnik 2017). A retrospective look at the history of using facts in democratic politics, however, indicates that the contemporary understandings and outcries about the post-truth age are hyper-sensational and idealistic. In politics, distorting, bending, stretching, moderating, or appropriating facts and evidence for public consumption have always been practiced in political deliberations, both democratic or non-democratic.

Public consumption of facts and evidence (acquired or experienced) goes beyond the control and mandate of the scientific knowledge enterprise. The enterprise's scope is limited to describing and explaining (positivist approaches) or constructing and interpreting (post-positivism) reality through producing evidence and facts. The utilisation of the discovered or constructed facts within domestic and international political arenas is a political process that contextualises, configures, or appropriates facts for public consumption. The *Social Studies of Science* (2017) refers to such a process as the configuration of the practices, discourses, and epistemic politics of modern facts. Studying the history of the modern facts, Poovey (1998) explains that facts need to go through a complex configuration with educational and government agendas to look more credible. In the contemporary world, even the hard facts related to environmental issues and catastrophe are appropriated and politicised by juxtaposing them with a politicised deep geological past that is likely to be confusing and forgettable (Davis 2016, 25).

Retrospectively, in international relations, the politicisation, configuration, and appropriation of facts for serving political agendas have existed since the Enlightenment. Therefore, facts, reality and truth have hardly been apolitical. On the contrary, they have been used as raw material for constructing discourses and legitimising power and oppression. European imperial and colonial powers formulated discourses based on distorted facts, lies, and deceptions to shape public opinion in their political domains. They were not concerned with telling the truth but with their interpretation of the truth (Du Bois 1946, 24). They went to the extent of holding their version of truth and facts as representations of nature. From misrepresenting and twisting the notion of natural law, the history of which goes as back as to ancient human civilisations (Neff 2003), to the reducing the state of nature to man's nature and reducing the latter to the good-evil dichotomy (see Hobbes 2011; & Locke 1986), the Enlightenment thinkers carelessly but confidently messed with the 'truth'.

In service of Western imperial and colonial agendas, the Enlightenment thinkers relied on empirical or fact-based validation to construct abstractions that could justify and rationalize violence and subjugation. For example, the abstraction of sovereignty, a contested notion in the contemporary globalized world, was formulated to rationalize the violence against the 'illegitimate' and invisible non-state people (Krishna 2006). Beyond literal meanings, such abstractions contain legal, moral, or political tropes for codifying societies. These are anything but objective, factual, or truthful classification criteria, and schemes. Indeed, ideological, moral, and even pseudoscientific imperatives were packaged and configured as facts and truth for advancing power agendas. Such falsifications were, and still are, needed for influencing Western public opinion about legitimising endeavours undertaken by their states and governments. The philosophical and intellectual foundations for such fabrications were provided by the very Enlightenment ideas such as Locke's government by consent and natural rights (Locke 1986); Kant's metaphysics of morals and perpetual peace (Kant 1983); Mill's promotion of happiness (Mill 1963); and Cobden's natural harmony of interests, to name a few.

Enlightenment era ideas, such as equality of citizens, limited state power and property rights, served Western societies and their domestic politics. These ideas became instruments for European powers to legitimise violent imperialist and colonialist agendas by constructing discourses grounded in unscientific and untruthful ideas. For example, while Kant promoted 'republic constitutionalism' in the Western world, his pro-slavery and culturalist ideas of mental and cultural incapability of native Americans, Indians, and Africans gave imperialist powers all the [pseudo]intellectual and moral reasons to justify their imperialist endeavours and brutal oppressions in those lands. Similarly, Mill's unscientific construct of promotion of happiness, and his pseudoscientific classification of non-European as barbarians and savages provided European powers with intellectual and moral contents to justify their brutal practices elsewhere under the discourse of civilising barbarians and savages. Even Mill's idea of non-intervention within and among 'civilised' nations was to effectively create internal harmony among these powers to implement their outward expansionism.

Against the backdrop of Enlightenment thoughts, the news, oral stories and published materials from non-Western colonised or occupied territories presented the Western audience with moral and intellectual reasons to justify Western interventions. They, therefore, legitimised the brutal practices of oppression and domination of their states as it seemed a burden over their shoulders to 'humanise' the 'less human'. The sources of such a mandate were nothing but the very reasons, morals, facts, truths and knowledge fabricated by Enlightenment thinkers. In brief, the intellectual revolution of the era, on the one hand, domestically helped Western societies in terms of subjecting government power to public opinion and consent. On the other hand, it enabled the same powers to construct discourses based on fabricated facts and truth orchestrated by intellectuals to legitimise oppression and brutality.

As a result, the Enlightenment era provided intellectual materials for forming a highly stratified and racially driven and codified international society. The Western powers and their public were unanimous about the subjectivity of [non-European] races to be ruled and about the well-deserved and earned right of the [European race] to rule and expand its rule beyond its own domain (Said 1995, 30). Therefore, in addition to having controversial racial histories, the thinkers of the Enlightenment were instrumental in shaping public opinion via untruthful facts. By doing so, these thinkers served as enablers in legitimising European violence and repression. Hence, post-truth is not an ahistorical contemporary phenomenon but a historical one which goes as least to the onset of the modern age, the age of reason and Enlightenment.

Similarly, since the end of the Second World War, fabricated facts and overstretched truths have been influential in defining power dynamics and the relationships between the Western powers and 'the rest'. To advance their international agendas Western powers package distorted facts and truths within constructed discourses with moral and normative appeals for the domestic audience. Modernisation, development, freedom, security, globalisation, democracy, terrorism and other such terms are examples of discourses that have been shaped and presented as objective facts and undeniable truths for stratifying international society. The main instrument for the Western powers to disseminate fabricated facts and untruths is through the media.

Conventional media is an integral part of this enterprise that furthers the discourses by adding additional layers and contents. From the colonial era, including during the professionalisation period of journalism in the early 20th century, media has routinely used hoaxes, sensationalism, and exaggeration (Finneman and Thomas 2018, 1–12). In addition to serving specific ideological and strategic goals, the media also has an economic incentive in promoting and disseminating constructed discourses. Using hoaxes, sensationalism, and exaggeration has remained means of selling newspapers from colonial times to today (Fedler 1989). So, if lies, deceptions, and untruths have been shaping public opinion since the beginning of the modern era, why is the concept of post-truth now becoming a lexicon in political science and international relations?

Post-truth or the end of a monopoly?

In the current age, the problem is not the invention of the post-truth political malaise but the dissolution of monopoly over the means of constructing discourses and their subsequent propagation. Since the Enlightenment, such a monopoly was in the hands of states machinery and mainstream traditional media. The populace was only at the receiving end to consume or recycle the presented discourses containing lies, fabrications, and untruths. With the democratisation (or proliferation) of information production and dissemination tools, the one-way top-bottom dynamic of manufacturing and dissemination of discourses has drastically transformed. Popular and alternative information creation and dissemination sources have become relevant, significant and influential in today's world. This has challenged the authoritative grasp and monopoly of elite sources, including the mainstream media, over the production, configuration, and dissemination of facts. Such a challenge has caused the emergence of the current alarmist narratives about post-truth politics. Among others, the proliferation of social media is crucial in challenging the domination and monopoly of political and ideological elites to influence and shape public opinion on given issues.

This change has three main aspects. First, with the proliferation of social and alternative information sources, the domain of discourse formulation and dissemination has diffused to the public sphere. Referred to as the universalisation of symmetry or the democratisation of epistemic (Fuller 2016), the monopoly over influencing and shaping public opinion is no longer the exclusive enterprise of the government and conventional media. Now the populace has platforms and tools to construct discourses and shape the opinion of their own kinds. Secondly, this democratisation subjected politics and power structures, mainly in democratic societies, to polarised public scrutiny through (mis)informed reflection shaped by alternative sources. Thirdly, and perhaps the most crucial but overlooked aspect of the post-truth age, is the changing relationship between the populace and the mainstream/ conventional media.

The popularity of the alternative means of information over the mainstream may not necessarily mean denial of facts or science, but the rejection of master narratives and discourses channelled from (mostly) mainstream media sources. Polarised public opinion may not indicate rejecting specific policy but resisting political discourse channelled from ideologically oriented mainstream sources, including media, corporations, and networks. Farrell (2015, 373) found that the increase in the climate change contrarian/denialist materials in five US media sources from 1993–2013 was not directly the rejection of climate change but the attached discourses. The study revealed that networks and corporations successfully influence the production and dissemination of denialist discourses, as they have broader interests in the privatisation of science and the influence of corporate lobbying around scientific issues (Farrell 2015, 373). As such, the public scepticism or rejection of media and corporate discourses does not imply the rejection of facts and science. Boussalis and Coan (2016, 98) found that relative to arguments against climate policy, the amount of denialist materials against mainstream climate science has increased since 2009. The study concludes that scientific scepticism often has political roots. This indicates that the polarised popular approach in the post-truth age is not necessarily against facts or truth but against monopolising facts and truth by elites, establishments, corporations and mainstream media.

The hyper-sensationalism about post-truth politics does not indicate the emergence of a new age in the relationship between the public and the truth. It is about the diminishing monopoly of conventional sources over controlling the construction and dissemination of master narratives. On the contrary, alternative sources effectively sway public opinions away from the mainstream influence on different issues. In such an antagonistic epistemic milieu, when the proliferation of epistemic sources and spaces disrupts the realisation of 'informed public reflection' on issues related to public and global policies, what challenges are there for epistemic communities.

The Challenges of Epistemic Communities in the post-truth Age

In the age of post-truth, the epistemic communities approach to policy enterprise has practical challenges. These challenges, however, stem from the epistemological foundation of the approach, which is at a crossroads of constructivism and empiricism. Hence, before discussing the practical challenges, it is helpful to review its theoretical limitations.

Theoretical challenges

Constructivism challenged the fundamental tenets of the positivist IR paradigms. However, before the emergence of constructivism, the positivist tradition experienced an internal rift by reconceptualising the assumption of facts as natural. Thomas Kuhn, in his *Structure of Scientific Revolutions*, rejected correspondence theory – which claims that true statements correspond to facts about the world (Hacking 2012). The theory was fundamental in shaping the logical empiricist International Relations approaches that inferred conclusions about the nature of the international system from the overarching ontological assumptions such as 'nature of man' and 'man in nature'. Subsequently, constructivism reconsidered the fabric of facts and reality, which led to redrawing the fundamental theoretical premises of international politics and governance.

As an IR theory, constructivism discusses the role of ideas and structure in shaping world politics by redefining relationships between actors. While ideas shape the meaning and structure of material reality through interpretation, structures give the agents autonomy to interact with others inside the structure to reshape the structure (Wendt 1999). This challenged the fixed nature of actors' interests, leading to restrained manoeuvrability in their behaviour on the international stage. Within the 'ideas' and 'structures' theoretical premises of constructivism, epistemic communities offer a model in which state and non-state actors construct their political realities through the knowledge provided to them by the experts. These actors formulate their interests and reconcile differences of interests (Haas 2015, 13). Haas argues that in their efforts to ameliorate uncertainty surrounding unfolding issues and hold some reality or truth about them, policymakers would turn to epistemic communities for knowledge. The communities will bring their knowledge-based interpretation of their casually informed version of reality and validity (Haas 1992, 21).

This account of reality and truth is embedded in constructivist epistemology, which argues against the 'true' existence of reality out there in the social world (Holznere and Marx 1978). However, by claiming an authoritative claim to policy knowledge, epistemic communities' epistemic attitude converges toward positivist orientation. While constructivism conceptualises reality as socially constructed and is suspicious of the existence of objective reality, the epistemic communities approach monopolises its construct and interpretation to a close expert circle. Haas argues that the communities do not necessarily generate truth (Haas 1992, 23). However, monopolising the construct of reality to experts is not compatible with the fundamental premises of constructivism. As such, while originating from constructivist epistemology, epistemic communities as an elitist approach re-introduces policy enterprise to empirical orientation. In the post-truth age characterised by the proliferation of epistemic sources and spaces and a hyper-polarised political struggle for dominance within the domain of policymaking, such a monopoly over the construction and interpretation of reality is counterproductive. Instead of offering a solution, epistemic elitism further polarises the struggle for authority and dominance within policy and knowledge enterprises.

Policy enterprise, by nature, is in a dialectic tension between knowledge and politics (Torgerson 1986, 33–59). This tension was crucial in derailing the public policy field from its initial envisioned post-positivist and democratic epistemological orientation towards empirical enterprise (DeLeon and Vogenbeck 2007, 3). The latter is characterised by the objective separation of facts and values (Fischer 2007, 223). As a result, the empiricist orientation introduced epistemological and methodological limitations to public policy enterprise, including over-generalising facts to non-related contexts. Initially, the facts-values paradox prompted the overlooking of political and social values that could not be translated into brute facts or pure scientific ends. As a result, the paradox practically distorted the effectiveness of the policy field for much of its evolutionary age. Rigorous quantitative analyses did not prove practical for social problems. With the shift of policy enterprise to post-positivism, the facts-values paradox seemed to resolve by reconciling empirical and political ends. However, the epistemic communities approach revives the facts-values paradox by pushing policy enterprise into the empiricist-constructivist epistemological juncture. It designates exclusive circles to reside over constructing facts, reimaging values, and, hence, shaping public policy as an exclusive expert or elite-oriented policy enterprise.

Such an epistemological realignment of public policy is not a solution but a problem in the post-truth age, characterised as the democratisation of the epistemic. In such a contested milieu, claiming expert authority cannot overrule the significance and relevance of other sources of authority claimed by other actors such as moral authority by activist and advocacy groups, or delegated and institutional authorities of elected officials and technocrats. As such, to claim exclusive expert authority in the age of post-truth is to conspire with political elites to monopolise facts and truths. The monopoly of expert and political elites over facts and reality production is not a novel idea, but a tradition that has been in practice at least since the Enlightenment, where intellectuals created norms, morals, ideas, and knowledge, and the imperialist and colonialist statesmen built upon them and created their own truths and realities about the world.

Practical Challenges

Given its elitist orientation, a question arises about the functionality of epistemic communities in the realm of democratic politics in the post-truth age. How can expert communities influence public opinion that socialises within unconventional and alternative epistemic spaces? The first practical challenge the approach faces in the post-truth age is its disconnect with democratic deliberations. The elitist orientation of epistemic communities to dominate policy enterprise contradicts the competition and pluralism principles of democratic deliberations.

In democratic settings, competition between actors is integral to policy processes. These processes are undertaken in a crowded and contested field of actors who claim different sources of authority and legitimacy to influence policy proposals and outcomes. In addition to expert authority, delegated, institutional, or moral are sources of authority in the policy arena (Sending 2015). This shows that scientific reasoning is only one instrument among many means of influence and reasoning at the disposal of different actors to advance their ideas and interests. Pluralism is another characteristic of democratic policy deliberation incompatible with the epistemic communities' expert-centred approach. Public participation is crucial for policy initiatives and a core normative value in functional democracies (Fischer 2002, 01). To realise this, public opinion (directly or indirectly) in policy deliberations is an unavoidable condition, and elected officials are entitled to moral, delegated, or institutional authority by virtue of representing people. Within the contemporary political landscape, socio-cultural, ideological, and identity-related values and discourses are crucial in defining and shaping polarised public opinion and perspectives. Opinions on given issues, domestic or global, shape a unique character of contemporary democratic politics – the rise of both right and left populistic orientation to public policy. Epistemic communities, claiming to offer an apolitical instrumentalist approach to policy processes, are impractical options whilst policymaking is becoming more politicised.

In the post-truth age, the malleability of public opinion to emotional appeals and personal beliefs should not, and cannot, defy the public deliberation principle of policymaking in democratic settings. While the functionality of democracy is linked with well-informed citizens (Kuklinski et al. 2000, 790– 816), misinformed or ill-informed reflections on policy issues cannot override the principle of public participation. More importantly, with the emergence of post-positivist approaches to knowledge and reality, the notion of informed or ill-informed became more subjective to meaning and interpretation. This challenges the legitimacy of the elitist authoritative claim to policy knowledge. In general, these limitations point to a gap in dialogue and communication between epistemic communities and democratic politics. By relying on scientific language, experts may not convince a politician whose arguments may be focused on public interest or opinion.

The second practical challenge is that the instrumental rationality of epistemic communities is incompatible with the bounded rationality that drives policy practices. Epistemic communities hold expert knowledge as an exclusive means to policy ends. Policy practices, on the contrary, are driven by 'bounded rationality' which is defined as incomplete human understanding of social phenomena due to limited cognitive, attentive, or scientific factors that drive policymakers to be part of a given problem at the expense of others (Andrews 2007, 161). As such, such a tension weakens the robustness and practicality of the epistemic communities' authoritative claim to knowledge.

The expert-focused approach of epistemic communities reinforces the challenges for its practicality in post-truth politics. Focusing exclusively on instrumental rationality as the means of influence overlooks the significance of dialectic/communicative discourses and participatory action practices of democratic politics and policy deliberations. Communicative rationality makes the democratic policymaking processes contested with dialogue and argumentation to reach a consensus. Rather than merely scientific, such argumentation is based on various discourses – normative, socio-cultural, ideological, and identity. In addition, communication and interactions are necessary conditions in policy deliberation. It not only contextualizes rationality but also validates normative rightness, theoretical truth, and subjective truthfulness (Habermas 1992, 28–57). In the post-truth age, in addition to scientific facts, these three elements of mental processes are crucial in driving public opinion. As such, the role of these elements in domestic policy deliberations has become substantive. They shape perspectives and public opinion.

Communicative rationality is a widespread practice within democratic policymaking processes. Epistemic communities, by offering policy solutions from a highly centralised and elitist source, on the contrary, is an authoritative approach and is incompatible with dialogue and argumentation. Focusing exclusively on instrumental rationality as the means to influence, the approach overlooks other practicing communicative discourses and participatory action practices of democratic politics.

A fundamental epistemological assumption of constructivism holds human agreement on social facts independent from the voluntary contract between actors. On the contrary, the exclusive contract between experts and policymakers that excludes public and democratic deliberations prevents epistemic communities from transforming into structures capable of offering language and meaning for generating agreement. Furthermore, in the age of post-truth, characterised by the proliferation and dissemination of sources of inferring meaning, any efforts to monopolise processes of inference and interpretations in the hands of experts are counterproductive. It further pushes public opinion on facts, reality, and truth towards novice alternative sources and spaces. This can happen as a reaction against pushing policy enterprise further away from democratic deliberations toward the expert-policy nexus.

Furthermore, global policy's uncertain and complex nature challenges epistemic communities' claim of authoritative expert knowledge. Paradoxically, given the changing nature of global issues, such a claim seems subjective and unsubstantiated. For instance, about global immigration, in an intellectual and scientific milieu, where different studies of various disciplinary nature and at different analytical levels suggest conflicting impacts of immigration on a national economy – what authoritative knowledge can a given epistemic community offer to policymakers? Similarly, the authoritative claim to knowledge cannot be objectively verified when globalisation and its master discourse of neoliberalism affect and transform contemporary social and economic issues differently in different socio-economic and political contexts. As such, any authoritative claim to facts and reality lacks objectivity and rigor and is more inclined to secure dominance and primacy in a contested global policy milieu crowded with different actors claiming various types of authorities.

Lastly, the increasing complexity of domestic and global issues confounded by the prevailing manifestation of post-truth politics necessitated an additional task in the policy enterprise – public education and learning. The task of scientific policy professionals would be to provide technical information for problem-solving and combine it with a new function of facilitating public deliberation and learning (Fischer 2004, 21–27). Fischer proposes that public deliberation and learning are highly relevant to domestic and global issues of democratic politics to expand and enable popular participation and informed reflection in the policy process.

With the polarisation of public opinion on domestic and global issues, policy formulation and making processes have become more contested by a struggle between science and politics or facts and values. In addition to competing for authority and power within these processes, the need for the contemporary science-based policy intermediaries – including expert networks and think tanks – to facilitate transferring learnings, communicating knowledge, and fostering public debate on policy issues and solutions to the grassroots multiplies. In its expounding, the epistemic communities approach mostly overlooks these undertakings in policy-related practices. While the role of science and facts in policy endeavours is becoming more crucial in a time identified as post-truth, focusing exclusively on the experts-politicians dynamics excludes an increasingly crucial element from the nexus – the significance and the role of informed public reflection.

Conclusion

Contemporary narratives on post-truth alarm us about the emergence of a new age in the relationships between truth and public opinion. These accounts describe the post-truth age as a circumstance in which emotions and beliefs are more effective in shaping public opinion and political actions than facts and truth. However, in the realm of international relations, objectivity, pure facts, and the truth of reality do not often have the currency for informed reflections. On the contrary, since the Enlightenment, untruths, distorted realities and fabricated facts have enabled Western powers to domestically shape public opinion to justify their inflicted injustices, oppressions, and brutalities elsewhere. The current hype about post-truth in Western societies has less to do with facts and science but more with a dissolving monopoly of power circles – political establishment and mainstream media – over constructing and disseminating master narratives and discourses. The proliferation of alternative epistemic sources and spaces has provided the populace with instruments and tools to construct and disseminate their own narratives about given issues. Such epistemic democratisation pushes public policy endeavours on domestic and global issues towards a populist orientation. Accordingly, having a pure scientific orientation, epistemic communities approach to public policy seems promising in counteracting the post-truth politics both in domestic and global policy arenas. However, the approach has theoretical and practical limitations in effectively shifting policy practices from populist toward scientific socialisation.

The post-truth age reinforces epistemic communities' challenges to be an effective and transformative policy approach. Its expert-centred epistemic practices are not aligned with some crucial aspects of policy processes in a democratic setting. The elitist orientation defies the competitive and pluralistic nature of democratic policy practices. Furthermore, the instrumental rationality of the approach is not compatible with the practical 'bounded rationality' of public policy. In the post-truth age, instrumental rationality is far from having an authoritative command on peoples' perspectives, perceptions, and understandings shaped by emotional appeals and personal beliefs.

With the spread of populism, where emotions and beliefs shape public opinion and political actions – and where the arguments of politicians are centred exclusively on public opinion – the scientific nature of the language employed by epistemic communities may not be convincing. Such divergence creates a strategic gap in dialogue and communication between epistemic communities and democratic politics. Lastly, as post-truth politics is characterised by being informed by polarised and ill-informed public opinion, epistemic communities' approach to policy offers no initiatives to facilitate an informed public reflection on policy issues through public deliberations and learning. By offering an exclusive expert-policy nexus, epistemic communities overlook the significance of communicating knowledge and fostering public debate on policy issues.

References

Bergmann, Eirikur. 2020. 'Populism and the Politics of Misinformation'. *Safundi* 21(3): 251–265.

Boussalis, Constantine, and Travis Coan. 2016. 'Text-mining the Signals of Climate Change Doubt'. *Global Environmental Change* 36, 89–100.

Burrell, Gibson, & Gareth Morgan. 1985. *Sociological Paradigms and Organizational Analysis: Elements of the Sociology of Corporate Life.* Routledge.

Clinton J. Andrews. 2007. 'Rationality in Policy Decision Making' in Frank Fischer et al. (ed), *Handbook of Public Policy Analysis: Theory, politics, and methods.* CRC Press.

Cross, Mai'a. 2013. 'Rethinking epistemic communities twenty years later'. *Review of International Studies* 39 (1): 137–160.

Davies, Jeremy. 2016. *The birth of the Anthropocene.* (2017). California. University of California Press.

DeLeon, Peter, and Danielle M. Vogenbeck. 2007. "The Policy Sciences at the Crossroads' in Frank Fischer et al. (ed). *Handbook of public Policy Analysis: Theory, politics, and methods.* Florida. CRC Press.

Denzin, Norman. 2001. *Interpretive Interactionism.* 2nd Edition. London. Sage Publications.

Douglas Torgerson, Douglas.1986. 'Between Knowledge and Politics: Three Faces of Policy Analysis'. *Policy Sciences* 19 (1): 33–59.

Du Bois, Willian Edward Burghardt. 1946. *The World and Africa: An Inquiry into the Part Which Africa has played in World History.* New York. International Publishers.

Editorial. 2017. 'Post-truth?' *Social Studies of Science* 47(1): 3–6.

Farrell, Justin. 2015. "Network Structure and Influence of the Climate Change Counter-movement." *Nature Climate Change* 6: 370–74.

Fedler, Fred. 1989. *Media hoaxes*. Ames, Iowa: Iowa State University Press.

Finneman, Teri, and Ryan J. Thomas. 2018. 'A Family of Falsehoods: Deception, Media Hoaxes, and Fake News'. *Newspaper Research Journal* 39(3): 350–361.

Fischer, Frank. 2000. *Citizens, Experts, and the Environment: The Politics of Local Knowledge*. Durham and London: Duke University Press.

Frank Fischer. 2004. 'Professional Expertise in a Deliberative Democracy'. *The Good Society* 13 (1): 21–27.

Frank Fischer. 2007. 'Deliberative Policy Analysis as Practical Reason: Integrating Empirical and Normative Arguments' in Frank Fischer et al. (ed), *Handbook of Public Policy Analysis: Theory, politics, and methods*. London: CRC Press.

Fuller, Steve. 2016. 'Embrace the Inner fox: Post-Truth as the STS Symmetry Principle universalized. Social epistemology Review and reply Collective'. https://social-epistemology.com/2016/12/25/embrace-the-inner-fox-post-truth-as-the-sts-symmetry-principle-universalized-steve-fuller/

Glanzberg, Michael. 2021. 'Truth'. *The Stanford Encyclopedia of Philosophy* (Summer 2021 Edition). Edward N. Zalta (ed.) https://plato.stanford.edu/archives/sum2021/entries/truth/.

Gopnik, Adam. 2017. 'Orwell's "1984" and Trump's America'. *New Yorker*, January 27.

Haas, Peter. 1992. 'Introduction: Epistemic Communities and International Policy Coordination'. *International Organization* 46 (1): 1–35.

Haas, Peter. 2016. *Epistemic Communities, Constructivism, and international Environmental Politics*. London/New York: Routledge.

Habermas, Jürgen. 1992. 'Themes in post-metaphysical thinking' (W. Hohengarten, Trans.). In *Post-Metaphysical Thinking: Philosophical Essays*. Cambridge: MIT Press.

Hacking, Ian. 2012. 'Introductory Essay' in *The Structure of Scientific Revolutions* (4th ed) by Thomas Kuhn. Chicago. Chicago: The University of Chicago Press.

Hobbes, Thomas. 2011. *Leviathan*. United States: Pacific Publishing Studio.

Holzner, Burkart, and John H. Marx. 1979. *Knowledge Application: The Knowledge System in Society*. Boston: Allyn and Bacon.

Kakutani, Michiko. 2018. *The Death of Truth*. New York. Tim Duggan Books.

Kant, Immanuel. 1983. *Perpetual Peace and Other Essays*. Translated by Ted Humphry. Cambridge: Hackett Publishing Company.

Kant, Immanuel. 2007. 'On the use of teleological principles in philosophy', translated by Günter Zöller. In *On the use of teleological principles in philosophy*, edited by Robert Louden and Günter Zöller. Cambridge: Cambridge University Press.

Kavanagh, Jennifer, and Michael D. Rich. 2018. Truth Decay: An Initial Exploration of the Diminishing

Role of Facts and Analysis in American Public Life. Santa Monica, California: RAND Corporation. https://www.rand.org/pubs/research_reports/pR2314.html/

Sankaran Krishna. 2006. 'Race, Amnesia, and the Education of International Relations'. In *Decolonizing International Relations*, edited by Branwen Gruffydd Jones. New York: Rowman & Littlefield.

Kuklinski, James, Paul J. Quirk, Jennifer J. Jerit, David Schwieder. & Robert F. Rich. 2000. 'Misinformation and the Accuracy of Democratic Citizenship'. *Journal of Politics* 62(3): 790–816.

Lakatos, Imre. 1980. *The Methodology of Scientific Research Programmes: Philosophical Papers, edited by* Gregory Currie, John Worrall. Cambridge: Cambridge University Press.

Lewandowsky, Stephan, Ullrich Ecker, and John Cook. 2017. 'Beyond Misinformation: Understanding and Coping with the "Post-Truth" Era'. *Journal of Applied Research in Memory and Cognition* 6: 353–369.

Locke, John. 1986. *The Second Treaties on Civil Government*. New York: Prometheus Books.

Mill, John Stuart. 1963. *The Collected Works of John Stuart Mill*, edited by John M. Robson. 33 vols. Toronto: University of Toronto Press.

Mill, John. 1977. 'Civilization' in *The Collected Works of John Stuart Mill*, edited by John M. Robson. Toronto: University of Toronto Press.

Neff, Stephen. 2003. 'A Short History of International Law' *in International Law*. 3rd edition, edited by Malcolm Evans. New York: Oxford University Press.

Poovey, Mary. 1998. *A history of the modern fact: Problems of knowledge in the Sciences of Wealth and Society*. Chicago: University to Chicago Press.

Popper, Karl. 2002. *The Logic of Scientific Discovery*. London: Routledge

Rosenau, James. 1999. 'Toward an Ontology for Global Governance' in Martin Hewson and Timothy J. Sinclair (eds.). *Approaches to Global Governance Theory.* New York: State University of New York.

Said, Edward. 1995. 'Secular Interpretation, the Geographical element and the Methodology of Imperialism' in *After Colonization: Imperial Histories and Postcolonial Displacements*, edited by Gyan Prakash. New Jersey: Princeton University Press.

Sending, Ole Jacob. 2015. *The politics of Expertise: Competing for Authority in Global Governance*. Ann Arbor: University of Michigan Press.

Stein, Arthur. 1990. *Why Nations Cooperate*. Ithaca, NY: Cornell University Press.

Wendt, Alexander. 1999. *Social Theory of International Politics*. Cambridge: Cambridge University Press.

10

Post-Truth and Post-Democracy: The Dark Side of the Democratic Planet

SILVÉRIO DA ROCHA-CUNHA AND RAFAEL FRANCO VASQUES

In one of his essays, the French social anthropologist Georges Balandier (1990) meditated on the paradigmatic transition that had been taking place during the late 20th century. He strongly emphasised that a necessary ethical evaluation of human actions has been forgotten, which should be based not only on the search for meaning, but also on a broader basis, which he called an anthropological basis. Only in this way would it be possible to compare and arrive at some principles common to all. However, Balandier draws attention to the fact that modernity has introduced fluidity and movement into social and political relations, where different times and values are opposed. And societies can ill afford indeterminacy. Man comes to live in a world where 'indifference, contempt, violence, can attack him at less cost, disquiet and fear make him more passive and the power of technology makes him malleable' (Balandier 1990, 5). This idea forces us to reflect on the true meaning of global politics in this digital age. Some authors have already spoken of a world deprived of meaning, others say that there is a sense of a world integrated into one history. However, there are several perspectives and controversies in today's world such as cosmopolitanism, pluralism and non-Western visions – each of which aim to explain and overcome the breakdown of sovereignty, interdependence within competition, and the need to overcome the logic of Westphalia despite the resistance of many of its assumptions, among other challenges. The contingent knowledge of political reality (Dussouy 2019, 172) has provoked contradictions: On the one hand, technical and economic achievement; on the other, an idea of linear and infinite progress that thinks it can overcome all limits. This fascination does not reduce, but rather amplifies, the restlessness of modern man who has conquered the rest of the world and partly imposed his political categories on it. All this translates into a growing entropy due to the increasing complexity of political systems – which does not favour the duty to judge that Hannah Arendt considered prior to any action (Berkowitz 2012).

Global politics carries within itself a deficient proportion between ends and means. This exacerbates social inequalities as well as exploits common goods and resources because the territories formerly regulated by states have come to be governed by a dense network of transnational interests. These are stripped of any local considerations because they correspond to a global mobility and profit criteria. Another important aspect that demonstrates the planetary chaos is the creation of what has been called 'types of men' who are measured exclusively by their function in this network. Some, such as famous athletes, appear as heroes, while others, such as migrants, appear as possible enemies or, in any case, as human beings deprived of moral recognition (Bayart 2004, 283) – which implies a deficit of civilisation (Balandier 2003, 29). These contradictions have much to do with another larger contradiction. Globalisation points in principle to a world subject to a universalisation of practices such as (for example) liberal democracy or the company as an essential agent or the market. At the same time, however, it fragments and radicalises cultures and needs sovereign states for wars that are to some extent infinite and without clear legal rules – maintaining the conflictual political structures that have always characterised Western civilisation. International relations definitively abandons the model of direct confrontation between the interests of sovereign states, partly because not all of the Westphalian model responds in a uniform way to the new international relations that are expanding to the rest of the world. This is partly because, as Badie (2020, 81) shows, conflicts undoubtedly continue – but around a social and economic fabric that raises global problems such as, for example, identity clashes and phenomena like inequalities derived from poverty and climate change, whose actors are transnational. However, this much larger scale, born with the global international system, increases tensions and uncertainty.

Here, we encounter a stumbling block of great importance. After the modern era went through a growing process of secularisation, immense contradictions have been added to the functioning of the political systems of the most developed countries – namely the legitimation crisis of political spaces that have always appeared as previously defined, the states. And, these suffer a strong erosion due to a global politics that is anchored in the functioning of markets that have become autonomous systems (Gauchet 2017, 670). One of the most important effects was the undermining of modern political culture, because it was based on the philosophies of history that had prevailed since the Enlightenment and became more acute during the political-international paradigm that Truyol y Serra (2004) called the 'world international system'.

When ideologically dominant, these philosophies of history (from Kant to Marx) always tended to proceed to a political unification of truth. With the decline of these narratives, it would have been possible to succeed an understanding of truth within objective frameworks – an understanding of the various levels, the multiplicities, the rhythms, that the quest for truth implies.

Finally, the contradictions of global politics are also based on the fact that modernity has exhausted the idea of a subject of rights and has come to consider man as a set of functional fragments. These are united through procedures that are not interested in the truth of existing, but rather in what is ceaselessly produced independently of the inter-subjective needs of each human being. In this way, the priority of the 'market system' (Romano 2004, 226) has the effect of a reified dependency that ignores choices relative to the formation of existential identity, leading to boredom and the triviality of existence itself. Time is 'looked at' but not 'lived'. The great promise of globalisation is therefore summed up in the assumption of the primacy of capitalist economic rationality and technological progress over political and cultural passions. This never happened because world order is a concept that implies many elements. As Sørensen (2016, 31) emphasises, 'world order is defined as a governing arrangement inside and among states, with the participation of other actors.'

Crisis of democracy, crisis of civilisation and post-truth

Between the logics of integration and the logics of power, the question of the nature of politics as a whole may arise. The crisis surrounding political action begins at the internal level of states. Some authors have called this problem the crisis of the spectacle state, the state of lies, the crisis of legitimacy. Crouch (2004, 35) calls it 'post-democracy', in the sense of having reached an extreme point in the 'democratic parabola' – that moment in which there is a great distrust on the part of important parts of society towards the institutions that govern, in which 'the very concept of government is placed in doubt' (Crouch 2004, 37). Crouch notes how this distrust is accompanied by a trivialisation of language in political communication, increasing discourse incapable of producing arguments that enlighten the public sphere, increasing sound bites around issues that are nevertheless of importance to a democratic society. Accompanying this increasing insignificance of the content of political discourse is also a polarisation of politics into personalities who show themselves as leaders expressing authority through non-rational artifices, reminiscent of non-democratic regimes. Therefore, Crouch sees the present moment as a form of regression from democracy as it was imagined in the early days of democratic ideas. Having been imagined does not mean that it has been realised, as we know, because liberalism had to pact with absolutism, restricting the ideals of the Enlightenment in a broad sense. For

Crouch what is happening is an attempt at a resurgence of elitist liberalism, albeit in new forms. This raises not only the issue of transparency and truth in political life, but also that of authoritarianism, which emerges as a solution to the mistrust of institutions.

Modern times, which have come to view politics as the management of scarce resources, have partly introduced lying at the heart of the exercise of power (think Machiavelli). Although a large part of political thought, especially influenced by Kant, continues to contest the legitimacy of falsehood in the exercise of power – considering that it prevents a true and productive communication between men, as well as propitiating the tendency towards arbitrariness of power in general (Cedroni 2010). We find this in Hannah Arendt (2021, 55), for example, who criticises the inability to judge in politico-military officials (during the Vietnam war) who are more prone to abstract and calculating analyses by anticipation, but whose truth has nothing to do with reality. For Arendt, lying is frequent because it focuses on a 'contingent reality' – a matter about which there is no 'intrinsic and intangible truth', and truth only becomes incontrovertible when it results from 'credible testimonies' anchored in solidly remembered memories (Arendt 2021, 15). This position accentuates Arendt's familiar position when she thinks of political action as a manifestation of human plurality.

The theme of truth has, however, come to be seen from other, more relative points of view. Vattimo stressed the relativism of truth, inserting the theme in his philosophy of 'weak thought', because, not recognising absolute truths typical of the positivism that dominated until the second half of the twentieth century, he never ceased to see the human as a manifestation of difference. It is for this reason that Vattimo notes that an entirely transparent society would be, if it were realised, a form of totalitarianism, defending instead a society whose freedom should be flexible and able to live 'diverse ways of life' (Vattimo 1990).

The problem of the relationship between truth and lies is, therefore, not simply an issue that has to do with so-called 'populism', but a problem that lies at the foundation of power. It becomes a moral problem (Cedroni 2010, 16) that can subvert the ethical-social relationship that legitimates the foundations of any political system. Cedroni considers that truth must be presented as objective, that it is right to believe what we consider to be true, that truth is an objective worthy of being questioned, that truth deserves to be cultivated for its intrinsic value. In this sense, the truth of democracy is, as Cedroni rightly defines it, 'a way of being of the political' (2010, 235). The political and philosophical positions that presuppose truth as essential to the proper functioning of a political system naturally consider that any instrumental deviation that deprives political action of truth will not be admissible. These visions do not include either deviation based on class interests or those that express any form of domination. This is a negative feeling towards those who occupy positions of political and economic leadership, even if elected democratically, and who are, for certain sectors of the population, in a somewhat fantastic way and without any proof of truth or lies, guilty of systematically lying and deceiving the people. This is an 'endless story' (Dupuis-Déri 2016), which has been translated either by disorganised social movements, or by masses who follow a leader who synthesises oppositional discourse.

Nowadays, such movements have been identified as new ways of looking at truth and lies in their relations with politics, more precisely as movements and opinion currents that convey what has come to be called post-truth. But these movements have a genesis of a theoretical nature, besides the fact that there is an abundant literature in the field of the sociology of communication and journalism that approaches the theme of post-truth as a novelty. Maurizio Ferraris (2019, 24) cites several books and articles that were published in 2017 this regard. But it is also a fact that some renowned authors debate the usefulness of the concept of post-truth because they consider it useless by virtue of the fact that post-truth is anchored in postmodernism and in the thought of Nietzsche – who asserted that there are no facts, but only interpretations. The Italian film director and writer Alessandro Baricco maintains that 'post-truth' explains nothing new and only serves as a justification for 'questionable behaviour and stupid ideas' and has turned out to be an idea that simultaneously expresses strong emotion and irrationalism that ends up serving political populism (2019, 25, 28). And it is equally a vehicle of simplification in the political domain. At the time of the 2000 US elections, Olivier Duhamel (2000, 22) noted that the constant gaffes committed by George W. Bush (such as: 'our imports come more and more from abroad') acquired force because they became a sign of sincerity, just as the error was proof of simplicity. Even then there was a detachment in a large part of the electorate, not only as regards knowing what the reality is, but also as regards knowing the truth itself.

Ferraris' idea (2019) that postmodernity has spread in the West in four phases seems correct: the first presupposed the idea of free spirits beyond good and evil; the second consisted in the appropriation of truth as a political weapon; the third, in the second half of the twentieth century, leaves truth aside because it was traumatised by the use that totalitarian systems made of truth, preferring morality, democracy or solidarity; the last has to do with what Ferraris calls the emergence of populist reason in political terms and the emergence of post-truth as a form of communicating, confused and horizontal, between rulers and ruled – where everything can be truth and its opposite. What, then, is the underlying problem? Ferraris points to a contradiction we have already alluded to. On the one hand, the conception of an idea of linear and infinite progress, the promise of a rationalised society in legal and political relations, and the promises of freedom, were accompanied by a legitimation of instrumental rationality. On the other hand, and in parallel, the modern era has been accompanied by reaction and revolt against this model of modernity, irrational and emotive reaction that turns to national identity, to tradition, to new mythologies and religions, communitarian impulses, etc. (Ferraris 2019, 33). The central issue lies in the contradiction between the realism of order and the ambition of principles. Since the Enlightenment, political theory has encountered this contradiction. As Margaret Canovan has observed, Rousseau's general will would make it possible to achieve the fundamental goal of justice, although this goal could only be attained through a solid feeling of solidarity. However, this feeling is only effective in relatively small and compact social systems, that is, when a particular social group manages to obtain legitimacy at the expense of excluding the rest of humanity. In short, the conflict between man and citizen is inevitable (Canovan 1998, 133). This is fertile ground for political decisionism and the decline of democracy.

Political decisionism was theorised by the German jurist Carl Schmitt and consists of the idea that decision, namely the decision by the state of exception, is the ultimate characteristic of sovereign power. Schmitt's ideas, directly or indirectly, aided the rise of the Nazi party during the Weimar Republic – insofar as they aimed at the idea of a strong state able to distinguish between friends and enemies and to guarantee stability and security within its political community. Sovereignty is thus expressed in the sovereign's ability to decide on a state of exception, that is, the power to suspend the legal order in force when faced with an exceptional case that is not foreseen in the legal order, in order to deal with an emergency situation for the integrity of the state (Schmitt 2009, 13–14). The entire political order is based on a decision and not on a norm – and sovereignty is characterised by concrete acts, such as the ability to decide what is meant by order or public security in the exceptional case. As an exceptional case cannot be foreseen, any attempt to limit it through the separation and balance of powers (as happens in the democratic rule of law) results in the emptying of the sovereign's power in the face of the emergency situation. This is why every decision-maker is, by definition, an authoritarian: they dismiss dialogue, compromise and the plurality that any democratic regime needs in order to stay intact.

Today, decisionism takes on new contours and supporters. On the one hand, populist movements call for the use of sovereign power under the figure of a strong leader, a kind of saviour able to restore order and lost identity, in the case of right-wing populism – or to bring about a radical transformation of societies in the case of left-wing populism. Both of these are linked by intolerance towards the idea of dialogue or consensus. On the other hand, we are witnessing a degeneration of democratic regimes into a kind of liberal authoritarianism that results in a 'permanent state of exception'. These demonstrate suspensions of rights, freedoms and guarantees by virtue of multiple emergency situations that tend not to cease – be they political, economic, social or environmental. As emergency situations have become the normality in contemporary societies, it is increasingly difficult for the public to scrutinise power. If we agree that democracy is, par excellence, the form of government where power must be permanently scrutinised and controlled, it is also clear that this new nostalgia for the return of sovereign power is fertile ground for the uses and abuses of lies. By this logic, it represents an instrument at the service of what Bobbio (2013, 27) has called 'invisible powers' – that is, those powers that make use of surreptitious, secret and even dishonest ways, without caring about truth or ethical issues and do so with a single instrumental purpose: the conquest of power.

Tensions between the unity of the true and the political in a global age.

Paul Ricœur (2001, 27, 51 and 187) reflected early, and with some wit, on the problem of truth and objectivity in human history and its political consequences. He began by distinguishing the objectivity sought by the natural sciences from the objectivity sought by the social sciences, namely history, and pondered the challenges that this distinction poses. Ricœur speaks of a necessary 'subjectivity implied by the expected objectivity' in historical research. There are, therefore, levels of subjectivity and the one that he defends is a subjectivity geared towards the thought of humanity – a 'subjectivity of reflection'. And it is in this way, by an approach through observation, whether of documents or traces of events, that a recomposition and reconstruction of the truth is carried out. This is always provisional, but it is simultaneously the foundation that sustains a more complete truth in the future. It is true that documents are always interpretable and evaluated by this purpose of committed subjectivity of the interpreter, but this performs an effort of ordering causalities that recover a version of history.

Therefore, there are conditions to be examined, although they are not necessarily decisive. At the same time, the truth of an event implies its recognition through the understanding of historical time, which permits 'to name the one that has changed, that has been abolished, that was another' (Ricœur 2001, 34), with the inherent difficulties. It is enough to evoke words like 'tyranny', 'servitude', or 'state' to realise that realities can be interpreted equivocally if they are not properly examined in their respective contexts with the due depth that the perception of time and place demands. Ricœur adds that the search for historical truth lies in the capacity to advance hypotheses for understanding the themes to be examined, without forgetting that all those who share a past and present history are part of the same history that they 'repeat' incessantly throughout time (Ricœur 2001, 37). And it will be in this interweaving of material documents and subjectivities with a will to understand, that one manages to avoid, argues Ricœur (2001, 39), hagiographies, inquisitorial imagination, the man of resentment, hatred. In short: as the historian Marc Bloch said, 'understanding is not judging'. To understand is not to judge because the search for truth, while uniting a man's subjectivity with his nature which develops historically, allows a true perspective. It also allows one to obtain the meaning of history itself. Ricœur gives an example in the figure of the philosopher Edmund Husserl, who recognised the 'meaning' of the West when he was confronted with the crushing of 'Socratic and transcendental philosophy' by Nazism (Ricœur 2001, 42).

These reflections allow us to reflect on several things. The first is that any history that reveals to us the true attitude of humanity at a given moment can never be as pure as has been argued above. There are always moments of irrationality where not all meaning is clear. The fact that society is historical means that human beings live under basic circumstances that force them to cooperate within conflict. That is why it makes sense to conclude, somewhat concretely and harshly, that individuals live in a very appreciable state of dissatisfaction – that in any society, the 'unfinished rational' reigns (Weil 1971, 93). Hence the characteristics mentioned before. The need for secrecy, traditions and mistrust of what is new are partly reactions that lead to conflicts and distortions in communication between individuals or political units. It is the job of culture to create models that point towards wider and freer horizons. However, the basic circumstances of human life, such as, for example, the scarcity of goods, the average utilitarianism of humans, the impossibility of each one possessing all the information available, among others, produce in social and political systems deformations in relation to memories. Thus, an undeniable tension persists between the sociability imposed by the articulation between institutions and other forms of cooperation between individuals and the natural historical individuality that remains in each individual. The secularised Western mass societies are, in these terms, mechanisms that crush the most particular values, at the same time as individuals reject many of the standards that somehow allow the subsistence of individuality. According to Weil, this mechanism of dissatisfaction within cooperation generates an important consequence in modern societies: the social system raises needs and goes about satisfying such needs to the exact extent that it replaces them with unmet needs. In Weil's words (1971, 99), 'necessity is both an evil which is eliminated by its satisfaction and the engine of good, of the satisfaction of needs', with the result that good is not really good, just as evil is not really evil. Both are to some extent outside the social horizon, introducing into each individual a sense of detachment from the organisation of the political system, seeking the pure 'morality' of imagined and imaginary communities.

The political field goes beyond formal political institutions. It is true that for Weil all political action must necessarily crystallise in the institutional form of the state, which represents the historically and politically organised community (Weil 1971, 131). And it could not be otherwise, because only with an organisation of this type would it be possible to claim to exercise a discourse with a reasonable sense and among human beings who, formally, are rational. In this way, Weil believes, the interests of the historical community and the actions of individuals, which are often irrational and instrumental, can be reconciled. In this sense, the role of education and the educator is relevant, because it is education in the context of a historical society that will determine a discourse that is at the same time reasonable and true. Weil attaches great importance to the ability of a society to be reasonable, where each individual will be the best he can be with whoever he is, and for this very reason he extends this dynamic to an idea of a world society composed of free states that adhere to it in order to satisfy the needs of reasonable individuals (Weil 1971, 240).

Weil's vision of modern society is rooted, as we have seen, in a tension between the needs of the individual and their complete satisfaction, which will never occur. And it is also rooted in the impossibility for an individual to take refuge in a kind of community that has also never been static and which is integrated in modern society that has transformed everything thanks to technology. It is true that Weil thinks that the point of sharing between the social mechanism and the individual will be what he calls 'living morality' (Weil 1971, 105) – a set of values that crystallises over time and is accepted in concrete terms. Although it must be said that a living morality will inevitably include various realities beyond the duties and obligations inherent in a social system (Hart 1996, 197). However, and as noted by Barcellona, modern technique 'tends to neutralise any possibility of constructing purposes that give meaning to human freedom' (Barcellona 2013, 32). From this simultaneously creative and destructive capacity emerges an individual who feels both atomised and insecure – integrated but without deep loyalty to the social system, deeply resentful and incapable of understanding the meaning of historical becoming. And, so, there has to be an entity that can unite these two forces: the growing rationalisation of society and the persistent dissatisfaction of the individual.

There is in Weil's thesis an unavoidable topic: modern society needs an entity that possesses the monopoly of legitimate violence – the state. It is obvious that the state has evolved, since the triumph of liberalism, into a constitutional state with separation of powers and which seeks to make power compatible with reasonable values within the framework of a pluralist society. It has evolved further: states have recognised the existence of an international community that shares minimum common values and pursues basic needs: freedom, collective security, satisfaction of the fundamental needs of the human race and, perhaps the maintenance of ecological balance. However, we can infer that in this quest around the problems that seek for truth, of which post-truth appears as an apparent opposite on equal terms, is placed in terms that are not abstract. We can access, says Ricœur (2001, 63), 'an intersubjective definition of truth according to which each one "explains" himself, develops his perception of the world in "combat" with another', whether in the past or in the present, in interaction that endlessly renews the points of view within a community of communication. Nevertheless, as we already know, this communication is not total, although it is equally certain that the idea of an absolute truth is a horizon to which humans aspire. The honest quest for truth requires a 'consonance' that cannot aspire to be a 'system' (Ricœur 2001, 67). Ricœur does not forget, however, a theme that we have already inferred from Weil, and which consists in the political problematic of the relative unity of the true. Relative unity, because it is empirical, suffers the twists and turns of history. The problem that arises is that of the necessarily violent unity of the true, whether religious or political.

Under what conditions can an organised human community respect all the principles that have so far been expressed? We already know that scientific and experimental truth has to set aside other truths, because one thing is 'man as the object of science', another is 'man as the subject of culture' (Ricœur 2001, 191). Therefore, Ricœur speaks of a triangle (perceiving, knowing and acting) in which each of the elements generates its own tension – dogmatising versus problematising – (Ricœur 2001, 192) and, as a result, succeeds in making truth 'vibrate'. However, this has not happened. Lies and fake news have begun to proliferate within social systems and at a global level. Yet, we are not facing the opposite of truth, but the perversion of the search for truth (Ricœur 2001, 216) through the use of manipulation techniques (Rodríguez Ferrándiz, 2018; García 2018; Le Goff 2002) that are placed on the plane of the simple 'technical' conquest of power. This social process has a paradoxically ancient side, because it places politics in the realm of opinion, of probability, of a determinist dialectic.

As has been explored across the chapters in this book, there is a lot of criticism of the new forms of mass media, such as social networks. However, in an open society such a criticism should make no sense (Cotarelo, 2012). This leads us to think that the problem lies rather in the absence of a dialogical dimension in the quest for truth (Cambier 2019, 147), one which is based on a relationship of cooperation and conflict – or 'ago-antagonisme' – a balance between positions of 'véridicité' towards the recognition of truth. There must therefore be much argumentation but following certain rules: a relationship between words and the world – the existence of a 'third party' that guarantees the existence of a commitment to dialogue and the relationship between words and the world, preventing the drift of argumentation. Finally, it is presupposed that there is consensus as to the purpose of obtaining the truth, since human language itself announces a 'telos' towards agreement (and here one could subscribe to a fundamental idea of Habermas' thought). The knowledge of truth depends, therefore, on the recognition of the interlocutors among themselves and of the context in which they act. Everything and everyone belongs to the 'set of admitted, inter-and transactionally constituted truths' (Cambier 2019, 156).

To not conclude: Does truth fit in a global society?

Throughout this chapter, we have shown that the relations between truth and post-truth are not ambiguous, but that post-truth tends to be a dissimulation of lies. Arendt, who always fought for pluralism, expressed strong reservations about an 'ideocracy' (as it appears in philosophy with Plato) which, with the pretension of a 'pure truth', does not allow the contrast of opinions. Against Strauss, who defended secrecy in government, Arendt counterposed truth as something to be obtained through a free political space populated by equal human beings. Only in this way would it be possible to escape a monological space typical of secret relations between states and, in domestic politics, typical of political action where rulers claim for themselves the truth even when masquerading as a noble lie (Jay 2014). This is why Arendt thought that the obsessive search for truth would always fall on the side of authoritarianism because it would end up eliminating the opinion derived from the first principle of political action: to use the word freely. Is it possible to re-engage discourse and politics based on the modern ethos? Quite possibly not. Perhaps what is needed is an ethos that proposes politics as a truly collective and free activity, capable of calling into question the imaginary of the really existing society – one that is capable of going beyond immediate interests.

This study was conducted at the Research Center in Political Science (UIDB/ CPO/00758/2020), University of Évora, and supported by the Portuguese Foundation for Science and Technology (FCT) and the Portuguese Ministry of Education and Science through national funds.

References

Arendt, Hannah. 2021. *Du Mensonge à la Violence. Essais de Politique Contemporaine*, tr., Paris: Calmann-Lévy, coll. Le Livre de Poche.

Badie, Bertrand. 2020. *Inter-socialités. Le monde n'est plus géopolitique*, Paris: CNRS Editions.

Balandier, Georges. 1990. 'Introduction. La Demande d'Éthique', *Cahiers Internationaux de Sociologie*, vol. 88, nouvelle série, 37.ème année, janvier-juin, 1990, pp. 5–12.

Balandier, Georges. 2003. *Civilisations et Puissance*, La Tour d'Aigues, Éd. de l'Aube.

Barcellona, Pietro. 2013. *L'Occidente tra Libertà e Tecnica*, Caserta: Edizioni Saletta dell'Uva.

Bayart, Jean-François. 2004. *Le Gouvernement du Monde. Une critique politique de la globalisation*, Paris: Fayard.

Berkowitz, Roger. 2012. 'The Burden of our Times', in Berkowitz, R. & Toay, T. N. (Eds.), *The Intellectual Origins of the Global Financial Crisis*, New York, Fordham University Press, pp. 1–13.

Bobbio, Norberto. 2013. *Democracia y secreto*, tr., México: FCE.

Cambier, Alain. 2019. *Philosophie de la Post-vérité*, Paris: Hermann.

Canovan, Margaret. 1998. *Nationhood and Political Theory*, Chelthenham UK/ Northampton, MA, USA: Edward Elgar Publishing.

Cedroni, Lorella. 2010. *Menzogna e potere nella filosofia politica occidentale*, Firenze, Le Lettere.

Cotarelo, Ramón. 2012. *El Sueño de la Verdad. Los Conflitos en la sociedad abierta*, Madrid: Ed. Catarata.

Crouch, Colin. 2004. *Posdemocracia*, tr., Madrid: Taurus.

Duhamel, Olivier. 2000. 'De l'a-démocratie en Amérique', in *Le Monde*, 11 November.

Dupuis-Déri, Francis. 2016. *La Peur du Peuple. Agoraphobie et Agoraphilie Politiques*, Québec: Lux Ed.

Dussouy, Gérard. 2019. *Le Pragmatisme. Outil d'analyse du monde*. Printed by Amazon.

Ferraris, Maurizio. 2019. *Post-vérité et autres enigmes*, tr., Paris: P.U.F.

García, L. 2018. *Choque de la Posverdad con la Democracia, el Poder* y la *Política*, Santo Domingo/Rep. Dominicana, Ed. Santuario.

Gauchet, Marcel. 2017. *L'Avènement de la Démocratie. IV – Le nouveau monde*, Paris: Gallimard.

Hart, Herbert. 1996. *O Conceito de Direito*, tr., 2nd ed., Lisboa: Fundação Calouste Gulbenkian.

Jay, Martin. 2014. *Le virtù della menzogna*, tr., Torino: Bollati Boringhieri.

Le Goff, Jean-Pierre. 2002. *La Démocratie Post-totalitaire*, Paris, Ed. La Découverte.

Ricœur, Paul. 2001. *Histoire et Vérité*, Paris: Ed. du Seuil, coll. Points.

Rodríguez Ferrándiz, Raúl. 2018. *Máscaras de la Mentira. El Nuevo Desorden de la Posverdad*, Valencia: Pre-Textos.

Romano, Bruno. 2004. *Fondamentalismo Funzionale e Nichilismo Giuridico. Postumanesimo, 'Noia', Globalizzazione*, Torino: Giapichelli Ed.

Schmitt, Carl. 2009. *Teología Política*, tr., Madrid, Ed. Trotta.

Sørensen, Georg. 2016. *Rethinking the New World Order*, London: Palgrave.

Truyol y Serra, Antonio. 2004. *La Sociedad Internacional*, 2nd ed., Madrid, Alianza Ed.

Vattimo, Gianni. 1990. 'Posmodernidad: una Sociedad Transparente?', in Vattimo *et al.*, *En Torno a la Posmodernidad*, Barcelona, Anthropos, pp. 9–19.

Weil, Éric. 1971. *Philosophie Politique*, 3rd ed., Paris: J. Vrin.

Note on Indexing

Our books do not have indexes due to the prohibitive cost of assembling them. If you are reading this book in paperback and want to find a particular word or phrase you can do so by downloading a free PDF version of this book from the E-International Relations website. View the e-book in any standard PDF reader and enter your search terms in the search box. You can then navigate through the search results and find what you are looking for. If you are using apps (or devices) to read our e-books, you should also find word search functionality in those.

You can find all of our books here: http://www.e-ir.info/publications

www.ingramcontent.com/pod-product-compliance
Lightning Source LLC
Chambersburg PA
CBHW050723030426
42336CB00012B/1398